JO PHENIX

The Spelling Teacher's

BOOK OF LISTS

Words to illustrate
spelling patterns
...and tips for
teaching them

Pembroke Publishers Limited

I dedicate this book to the teachers who, in many workshops and seminars, have helped me investigate words: in Canada, from Qualicum, British Columbia, to Cape Breton, Nova Scotia, and Timmins to Windsor, Ontario; in the United States, from Fort Yukon, Alaska, to Lake County, Florida, and San Jose, California, to Deerfield, Massachusetts; in Britain, Jean Ramsay and the teachers of Clywd, North Wales, and Jean Kilyon in Bradford, Yorkshire.

My very special thanks go to my sister, Judith Worsnop, and good friend Anne Goldthorpe, for their continuing support and friendship.

© 1996 Pembroke Publishers Limited
538 Hood Road
Markham, Ontario, Canada   L3R 3K9

Canadian Cataloguing in Publication Data

Phenix, Jo
  The spelling teacher's book of lists

ISBN 1-55138-066-8

1. English language – Orthography and spelling –
Study and teaching (Elementary).   I. Title.

LB1574.P54 1996   372.6'32   C95-932931-5

A catalogue record for this book is available from the British Library.
Published in the U.K. by
Drake Educational Associates
St. Fagan's Road, Fairwater, Cardiff CF5 3AE

Editor: Kate Revington
Design: John Zehethofer
Typesetting: Jay Tee Graphics Ltd.

Printed and bound in Canada by Webcom
9 8 7 6 5 4 3 2 1

Contents

Introduction

About This Book

The works of Shakespeare contain about 37 000 different words. Most of us do not use nearly this many in our writing. However, the average high-school graduate may use 30 000 words. The average 12-year-old knows about 12 000 words. Even people who consider themselves to be poor spellers can spell most of the words they need correctly.

We cannot expect to learn all the words we are going to need by memorizing them one at a time. There are too many, and our memories are just not that good. When we want to write a word, we do not search our memories for the correct order of letters. We call up our knowledge of patterns, and construct words as we need them. Doing this allows us to spell words we do not use often, and even many we have never seen before. The better our knowledge of the patterns in words, the fewer spelling mistakes we are likely to make.

Few words stand alone in our language.

Most words belong to spelling patterns based sometimes on the way they sound, sometimes on the ways they are used, and sometimes on their meanings and origins. This book illustrates some of the ways in which words are connected, and suggests an approach to spelling based on pattern recognition, meaning, and problem solving, rather than on memory.

This book does not attempt to provide a complete list of patterns or words which fit patterns. Rather, it is a starting point for investigations into words, both in the classroom and in our print-filled lives. You will personalize this book when you add your own words and your own discoveries.

A word of caution: The spelling patterns in this book have been compiled by an ear which has spent half its life in England, and half in Canada. As a result, my hearing of dialects has become a little blurred. We do not all hear words in the same way. Often, I make comments about the effects of dialect on pronunciation and spelling. Not only that: Like all Canadians I have to cope daily with differences in

British spelling and American spelling, and I am not sure how consistent my choices are. Something that complicates this further is the fact that Canadians are still ambivalent about which side of the Atlantic their spelling belongs to. The result is that many of the people reading this book will think I am making spelling mistakes when I write such words as *labeled* and *favourite*. Remember, there is no absolute right and wrong in English spelling, only a general consensus relative to where we live, where we went to school, and sometimes how old we are.

We all form our own connections, and develop our own spelling logic.

How to Use This Book

This book is not a program of instruction, and is certainly not a collection of word lists to study and memorize.

It is a personal collection of interesting words, patterns and facts about language. I have collected these words over a number of years of working with children and with many groups of teachers. Teachers at workshops have often asked, "What are the patterns we can investigate? What are the words we can use? How can we find out about patterns, rules, and exceptions?" This book is one answer to those questions.

The Spelling Teacher's Book of Lists is for our day-to-day work as teachers in the trenches, trying to help children make sense of spelling. Words are listed and categorized in ways I think are meaningful, based on experience of the kinds of spelling errors children make, and the kinds of thinking they do to figure out words. Our students will probably not become word experts. But perhaps they will begin to find their own logic and patterns, and develop workable methods for constructing words. We can hope that they will begin to find words interesting, and not objects to be feared.

Do not give these word lists to your students. They are here for *your* information and interest. When you look at the patterns illustrated, decide for yourself which are interesting, which will be useful for your students to know about, and which you will adapt for your own use. Please see this book as a resource of patterns and words to stimulate similar investigations in your own classroom. Students will learn more and be more interested if they make their own collections, form their own categories, and find their own patterns.

This book is for children and adults of all ages. Students do not learn the patterns of language in any predetermined sequence. Many older students have not made generalizations about spelling, and therefore cannot make good spelling decisions. Many adults spell poorly because they do not see spelling as a logical process of using patterns to construct words. Second-language learners often have difficulty with English spelling because they see it as illogical, even random. Learning spelling patterns is for everyone.

Writing for a real audience is the only purpose for standard spelling. The real test of whether we understand spelling is our ability to use our knowledge of patterns to construct the words we need for the real writing we need to do.

Building Spelling Patterns

Many of us find looking up a word in a dictionary hard, because along the way, we notice several other words we just have to stop and read about.

Curiosity about words is the starting point for spelling learning. If we are curious about words, we do not stop at just looking up the spelling of a word. We look at the origin, the derivations, and other related words listed before and after in the dictionary. Every time we do this, we are reinforcing for ourselves the fact that words are connected, and that knowledge about one word can give us information about the meaning and spelling of many other words. Good spellers use this kind of information when they write.

Reading and writing are often good places to start investigations into words. When we notice an interesting word in our reading, or are in doubt about how to spell a word, we should note the word for a closer look.

Making lists of words which share some element of spelling is a good idea. The act of making such lists helps us to focus on the patterns. Once we have done this, we will notice other words that we can add to our lists. Seeing words grouped together can often help us to remember that they are similar. The lists can become a resource to use for checking spellings.

Do not worry about finding every single example of a particular pattern. Those you do not think of or come across in your reading or writing over the course of several days are probably not very common. Once you become aware of a particular pattern, you will begin to notice words that fit and words that do not. You will often notice a new word many weeks after you have focused on a particular pattern; frequently, a word jumps from the page when you are reading, and triggers a memory of other similar words you have looked at before.

Never skimp on the collection of words to use as examples. You *cannot* generalize a spelling pattern from a few words. The more words you have, the more likely you are to spot the connections. Take several days, if necessary. Students can mobilize their families to contribute words.

Be wary about students using a dictionary to add words to a word list. Copying words from the dictionary is not necessarily a learning experience, especially if the students fail to understand the words. First, list as many words as the group can think of, then add those that appear in the normal course of day-to-day reading and writing. In this way, students will build patterns using words they know, understand, and are likely to use. They can then go to a dictionary to see if there are any more. Students may want to find out whether the words they thought of are the only ones that exist, or whether there are many more words that they do not yet know about. They may find derivations of words they know and thereby build their vocabularies.

The aim for spelling learners, whether children or adults, is to discover that patterns are there for them to find — and to use to build words they need in their writing.

What to Do with a Word List

Plan to keep the word lists you and your students build. Once students have spent time looking at a particular pattern, they will probably recognize it when they see it again. They may not remember all the words, but when they puzzle over how to spell a word, they may remember that it was on one of the lists they collected.

- Keep lists in a ring-binder for easy access.
- Ask a student to enter a new list into a computer. The list can be printed out as needed, and can be added to and updated throughout the year.
- Ask a student to alphabetize a list before storing it. Every time students look for a word on a list, they will be using the same skills they need to find words in a dictionary.
- When you have several lists, ask students to categorize them. The categories might be similar to those in this book, but often students group lists in ways that are more meaningful to them. Categorizing should make it easier for them to find any particular list.
- Revisit lists you have made before. You will do this to add new and interesting words you find. Students can use the lists as resources for writing, for the creation of riddles and rhymes, and for word games and puzzles.
- Encourage students to select words from the lists for their own reference. These might be words they have trouble spelling, words they find interesting and want to keep, new words they want to add to their writing vocabulary, words to take home for the family to talk about. A personal spelling journal is the ideal place for this.
- Keep a list of the patterns you have worked with. You can use it when you plan for next year. You can also use it as a checklist for assessment. From time to time, have it beside you when you read the students' writing, and check which of the patterns they are able to use successfully, and which they need to revisit.

1/Consonants

Consonants seem easier than vowels because the sounds they represent are usually more predictable. However, most consonant sounds can be represented in more than one way.

A consonant tends to sound the same whether it appears at the beginning, at the end or in the middle of words. You only have to learn the sound represented by a letter once. However, when you are collecting words, you may want to find examples of consonants in different places in words. Doing so can help students to listen to each part of a word when trying to spell it. Also, you will find that not all letter combinations can appear anywhere in a word; some never appear at the beginning or end of a word. This knowledge will cut down on the number of alternatives you have when spelling a word.

Some possible consonant spellings are very rare, sometimes found in only one word. Often they indicate the language of origin. If we need to use those words, we will have to remember them. Often reading them frequently and using them in our writing will allow us to remember them easily. We do not need to study them, but can keep an eye out for new uses for a consonant or consonant combination. You can draw children's attention to them when they crop up in their reading.

Some of the letter sounds represented here may not seem linguistically correct, but we do not always speak precisely and accurately. Early spellers rely on the way they hear sounds in order to predict spellings. Listening to the way children pronounce words can give us insights into how and why they determine which letters to use.

Ways to Spell Consonant Sounds

b	b	bb			
	banana	— — —			
	ca**b**in	ho**bb**y			
	tu**b**	e**bb**			

ckq	c	ch[1]	k	ck	qu
	cat	**ch**orus	**k**etchup	— — —	**qu**iche
	va**c**ation	e**ch**o	ma**k**ing	lo**ck**smith	mos**qu**ito
	ar**c**	lo**ch**	tre**k**[2]	lu**ck**	che**que**[3]
	cc	**cq**	**cu**	**cch**	**lk**
	— — —	— — —	— — —	— — —	— — —
	desi**cc**ate	ac**q**uire	bis**cu**it	zu**cch**ini	ta**lk**ing
	— — —	— — —	— — —	— — —	fo**lk**
	kh				
	khaki				
	— — —				
	— — —				

[1] Words in which **ch** has a hard **c** sound often come from Greek.
[2] Words ending in **k** without a preceding **c** are very rare in English. Perhaps this is the only one. *Trek* is borrowed from Afrikaans. The Great Trek was a historic migration of people in South Africa.
[3] This is a British spelling. In America this word is spelled *check*.

d	d	ed	dd	ld	dh
	danger	— — —	— — —	— — —	**dh**ow[4]
	ri**d**ing	— — —	a**dd**ition	shoul**d**n't	— — —
	han**d**	fill**ed**	a**dd**	coul**d**	— — —

[4] *Dhow* is an Arab word for a sailing vessel.

[5] There are a few names which begin with **Ff**, for example, Ffoulds.
[6] When an **f** sound is spelled with **ph** it usually indicates that the word has a Greek origin.

f	f	ff	gh	ph	lf
	fee	[5]	— — —	**ph**one[6]	— — —
	sa**f**ety	e**ff**ort	tou**gh**en	ele**ph**ant	ha**lf**way
	che**f**	ski**ff**	lau**gh**	gra**ph**	ca**lf**

g	g	gu	gue	gg	gh
	girl	**gu**est	— — —	— — —	**gh**erkin
	fin**g**er	life**gu**ard	— — —	e**gg**head	
	han**g**	— — —	synago**gue**	— — —	— — —

h	h	wh
	happy	**wh**o
	be**h**ave	— — —
	— — —	— — —

[7] *Raj* and *Haj* are probably the only words ending in **j** which are in use in English, although neither is really an English word.
[8] Note the pattern for using **ge** and **dge** on pages 41-42.

j	j	g	ge	dg	dge
	jam	**g**inger	**Ge**orge	— — —	— — —
	in**j**ure	refri**g**erator	coura**geo**us	ba**dg**er[8]	ju**dge**ment
	Ra**j**[7]	fri**g**	hin**ge**	— — —	bri**dge**

gg	dj	d
— — —	— — —	— — —
exa**gg**erate	a**dj**ust	sol**d**ier
— — —	— — —	— — —

k	*See **ckq***.

l	l	ll
	land	**ll**ama
	fee**l**ings	fi**ll**er
	stee**l**	fu**ll**

[9] When the **mn** are in the middle of a word, both the **m** and the **n** are heard (columnist, solemnity). This is one way of locating silent letters. For more on silent letters, see pages 26-28.

m	m	mm	mn	lm	mb	gm
	mother	— — —	— — —	— — —	— — —	— — —
	co**m**ing	co**mm**on	— — —	ca**lm**ing	cli**mb**ed	— — —
	far**m**	— — —	colu**mn**[9]	pa**lm**	to**mb**	paradi**gm**

chm
— — —
— — —
dra**chm**[10]

[10] A measurement of weight, the word heard more in Scotland than elsewhere.

[11] Mnemosyne was the Greek goddess of memory. Her name begins with the n sound. We find the same mn in *amnesia*, the loss of memory.

n	n	kn	gn	pn	mn
	not	**kn**ot	**gn**at	**pn**eumatic	**mn**emonic[11]
	ca**n**al	un**kn**own	si**gn**ing	_ _ _	_ _ _
	kee**n**	_ _ _	rei**gn**	_ _ _	_ _ _
	nn				
	_ _ _				
	a**nn**oy				
	A**nn**				

p	p	pp	gh
	place	_ _ _	_ _ _
	de**p**ict	a**pp**le	hiccou**gh**ing
	la**p**	_ _ _	hiccou**gh**

q	*See ckq*.

[12] In some dialects, an r at the end of a syllable is not pronounced; the words *father* and *farther* sound exactly the same. In most dialects the final r is hard for young children to hear, and therefore to spell.

r	r	rr	rh	wr	rrh
	rat	_ _ _	**rh**yme	**wr**ist	_ _ _
	hai**r**y	ca**rr**y	_ _ _	re**wr**ite	haemo**rrh**age
	fa**r**[12]	Ke**rr**	_ _ _	_ _ _	my**rrh**

s	s	ps	c	ss	sc
	sad	**ps**alm	**c**ircus	_ _ _	**sc**ience
	ri**s**ing	para**ps**ychology	ne**c**essary	mi**ss**ing	re**sc**ind
	ye**s**	_ _ _	_ _ _	ki**ss**	_ _ _
	sch	st	sw		
	schism	_ _ _	**sw**ord		
	_ _ _	ca**st**le	_ _ _		
	_ _ _		_ _ _		

t	t	tt	th	ght	ed	pt
	ten	_ _ _	**th**yme	_ _ _	_ _ _	**pt**eradactyl
	migh**t**y	se**tt**le	_ _ _	si**ght**ing	_ _ _	_ _ _
	mean**t**	bu**tt**	_ _ _	bou**ght**	stopp**ed**	recei**pt**
	bt	ct				
	_ _ _	_ _ _				
	de**bt**or	vi**ct**uals				
	dou**bt**	_ _ _				

[13] This is the only word which ends in **v**. It is really an abbreviation derived from *revolve*.

v	v	vv	f	ph
	van	— — —	— — —	— — —
	revise	revved	— — —	Stephen
	rev[13]	— — —	of	— — —

w	w	wh	u	o
	with	which	— — —	one
	coward	nowhere	question	choir
	snow	— — —	— — —	— — —

[14] Words that begin with **x** sound as if they begin with **z** (*xylophone*).

x	x	cks	cc
	x[14]	— — —	— — —
	mixing	— — —	accent
	six	sacks	— — —

y	y	u	ea	e	ie	i
	yes	ukelele	— — —	— — —	— — —	— — —
	saying	refuse	beauty	feud	adieu	view
	— — —	menu	— — —	— — —	— — —	— — —

z	z	s	ss	zz	x
	zoom	— — —	— — —	— — —	xylophone
	razor	closing	scissors	fizzy	— — —
	Oz	was	— — —	buzz	— — —

Double Consonants

In words of more than one syllable, a strong relationship exists between short vowels and double letters. Try collecting examples in themes.

DOUBLE LETTERS AFTER SHORT VOWELS					
adjectives	happy	messy	silly	jolly	funny
animals	rabbit	lemming	kitten	grasshopper	buffalo
clothes	?	leggings	mittens slipper	bonnet	muffler
verbs	grabbed	messed	kissed	bossed	fussed

DOUBLE LETTERS AFTER SHORT VOWELS — *Continued*					
cooking	batter apple carrot	pepper	simmer fillet	coddle coffee	butter buffet
at home	mattress	dresser doorbell cellar	pillow	cottage	burrow
garden	daffodil yarrow	?	zinnia willow	hollyhock	buttercup
games	batting	tennis	tiddlywinks	volleyball	shuffleboard

DOUBLE LETTERS BEFORE AN *LE* ENDING (These are all short-vowel words.)				
babble		dribble	hobble	bubble
paddle	meddle	middle	coddle	muddle
baffle		piffle		truffle
gaggle		giggle	toggle	struggle
apple		ripple	topple	
hassle				tussle
battle	nettle	little	bottle	scuttle
dazzle		fizzle	nozzle	guzzle

Here are two groups of words, all with similar endings added, following the more regular North American pattern. In the words on the left, we must double the final letter before adding the ending. In the words on the right, we must not. For a clue about the reason, as you read each list, note which is the stressed syllable.

DOUBLE LETTERS AND THE STRESSED SYLLABLE	
Last letter doubled	Last letter not doubled
ful**fill**ing con**troll**ed en**roll**ing ex**cell**ed dis**pell**ed	**quar**reling **lev**eled **can**celing **la**beled un**par**alleled
con**cuss**ed	**fo**cused
pre**ferr**ing	**off**ering

14

DOUBLE LETTERS AND THE STRESSED SYLLABLE — Continued	
Last letter doubled	Last letter not doubled
al**lott**ed	in**hib**ited
com**mitt**ing	pro**hib**iting
trans**mitt**ed	**me**rited
a**bett**ed	**co**veted
for**gett**ing	**ben**efited

As a general rule: When the stress is on the final syllable, double the last letter when adding endings.

Note how this pattern works in these words.

ex**cel**	ex**cell**ing	**ex**celent
pre**fer**	pre**ferr**ing	**pre**ference
con**fer**	con**ferr**ed	**con**ference
de**fer**	de**ferr**ing	**def**erence
re**fer**	re**ferr**ed	**ref**erence

In Britain it is the custom to double a final **l** or **s** no matter where the stress falls, giving us spellings like these:

[1] The spelling *focusing* is now also seen in Britain.

labelled	**ex**cellent	**can**celled	**fo**cussing[1]	**trav**eller

Excellent is the only one of these still common, but not universal, in the United States.

The North American pattern reflects how we change spellings to make them conform to a perceived pattern.

PRONUNCIATION NOTE

In North America, the word *harassed* is pronounced with the stress on the second syllable. It must be pronounced thus in order to fit the pattern. In Britain, it is pronounced either *harassed* or *harassed*.

SPELLING TIP: The following words do not fit the North American pattern above.

    outfitting   **wood**cutter

As compound words, they follow a different pattern — all the letters of the joined words are present.

out + fitting = outfitting   wood + cutter = woodcutter

DOUBLE CONSONANT ALPHABET

bb	cabbage	rabbit	fibber	stubble
cc	raccoon	moccasin	broccoli	zucchini
dd	sadder	sudden	fiddle	muddy
ff	gaffer	riffle	scoffing	scuffle
gg	haggle	stagger	biggest	muggy
hh	hitchhiker	withhold	fishhook	ranchhand[2]
jj				
kk	trekkie[3]			
ll	allow	dollar	well	filling
mm	hammer	lemming	dimmed	summer
nn	annoy	penny	finnicky	funny
pp	apple	ripple	hopper	guppy
qq				
rr	arrow	carrot	horrible	hurry
ss	hassle	lesson	kissing	fussed
tt	matted	letter	litter	clutter
vv	revved			
ww	powwow			
xx				
yy				
zz	jazz	dazzle	whizzed	buzzed

[2] **Hh** is possible only in compound words.

[3] Fans of *Star Trek* are the only ones who fit this category.

SPELLING TIPS: Words which logically should have **kk** are spelled **ck**. Words which sound as if they have **jj** have **ge** or **dge** instead. In most **cc** words, you can hear two sounds: *success, accept*. They are not really double-letter words, but roots plus prefixes.

Consonant Combinations

Consonants can combine in twos or threes, and very rarely in fours. In the combinations you can sometimes hear one letter (*choir*), sometimes two letters (*crust*), and sometimes three letters (*scrap*). Some combinations make an entirely new sound (*this*). Sometimes figuring out whether two consonants are a combination or one consonant and a silent letter (*which*) is difficult.

Note which combinations cannot be followed by every vowel. Note, too, which combinations can appear both at the beginnings and ends of words — and which cannot.

Two Letters — One Sound

All two-letter combinations that make one sound include the letter **h**. **Sh, th** and **ch*** are combinations called *digraphs*. They make one new sound, rather than the sound usually represented by one of the letters. **Wh** represents either **w** or **h**, and does not make a new sound. **Ph** and **gh** represent the sound of **f**.

sh	The sound usually represented by **sh** can be spelled in many ways.				
	sh	**ti**	**ci**	**ss**	**ce**
	shop	ac**ti**on	pediatri**ci**an	mi**ss**ion	o**ce**an
	fi**sh**ing	men**ti**on	suspi**ci**on	i**ss**ue	crusta**ce**an
	ca**sh**	pollu**ti**on	spe**ci**al	Ru**ss**ia	
	si	**s**	**ch**	**sch**	**sci**
	pen**si**on	**s**ure	**ch**andelier[1]	**sch**edule[2]	con**sci**ous
	man**si**on	**s**ugar	ma**ch**ine	**sch**ist	con**sci**ence
	ten**si**on	nau**se**ous	**ch**agrin		

[1] When **ch** sounds like **sh** it usually indicates that the word came from French, like *chauvinist* and *Charlotte*.
[2] The British pronounciation.

[3] Unless you count *thyme*, but you would probably consider the **h** silent.

th	This digraph has two different pronunciations[3]:			
	that	bathe	thank	bath
	the	breathe	theme	teeth
	this	with	thin	pith
	those	other	thought	moth
	thus		thumb	mouth
	thy	worthy		myth

* **Ch** also represents the sound of hard **c**, for example, in *choir* and *chemistry*. This is usually a sign that the word came from Greek.

[4] Beginning spellers often spell this sound with just **h**, because they can hear the right sound in the name of the letter.

[5] To choose correctly between **ch** and **tch**, see the pattern on pages 40-41.

[6] Children often pronounce *picture* and *pitcher* in the same way. Building both patterns might help them distinguish between the two.

ch	The sound usually represented by **ch** can be spelled in different ways[4]:

ch	tch	t	ti
chick	ca**tch**	pic**t**ure[6]	ques**ti**on
mar**ch**ing	ha**tch**et[5]	na**t**ure	
por**ch**			

wh	This usually represents the sound of **w**, and more rarely, that of **h**. In some dialects of English, particularly in Scotland, the **h** is pronounced as a breath of air along with the **w**. It is called an aspirated **h**, and the breath of the **h** is heard first.

A number of the most commonly used of these words can be listed and used as question words.

what	which	who	whomsoever
when	whichever	whose	
whence	wither	whoever	
where	why	whomever	

[7] When you look at your lists, you will discover that if **wh** is followed by **o**, you can predict it is likely to sound like **h**.

[8] You can pronounce *whoop* with either an **h** sound or a **w** sound.

You can build other patterns by following the **wh** with different vowels:

whack	wheat	whiff	whole[7]
whale	wheel	while	whocp[8]
wham	wheeze	whine	
wharf	whelk	whim	
	whelp	whimper	
	wherry	whine	
	whether	whinny	
		whip	
		whirl	
		whisk	
		whisker	
		whisper	
		whistle	
		white	

[9] An open, horse-drawn carriage.

[10] Now more usually spelled *fantasy*.

[11] The dictionary lists dozens of words with the prefix **photo**.

ph					
	phaeton[9]	pheasant	phial	phlogistic	phylactery
	phalange	phenacetin	Philadelphia	phlox	phylloxera
	phalanx	Phenix	philander	phobia	phylogenesis
	phantasm	phenobarbitol	philanthropist	Phoebe	phylum
	phantasmagoria	phenomenal	philately	Phoenician	physical
	phantasy[10]	phenomenon	philharmonic	Phoenix	physics
	phantom	phrenology	Philip	phone	physiognomy
	pharaoh		Philippines	phoneme	physiology
	pharisee		philodendron	phonetic	
	pharmaceutical		philology	phonics	
	pharmacist		philosophy	phonogram	
	pharmacy		philtre	phonograph	
	pharynx		phlebitis	phonology	
	phase		phlegm	phony	
	phrase			phosphate	
				phosphorus	
				photo[11]	

	graph	elephant	cipher	orphan	hieroglyphics
	grapheme			dolphin	
	epitaph			trophy	
	cacophony			endomorph	
	Epiphany			morpheme	
				Sophie	
				sophomore	
				prophet	

gh			
	laugh	cough	rough
	draught		tough
			enough
			slough

ETYMOLOGICAL NOTE

Many of the words with **ph** come from Greek. Note also how many of them have scientific, especially medical, meanings, since these sciences originated with the Greeks. Even in modern times, when scientists need to create new words, they often go back to Greek roots.

Two Letters — Two Sounds

	bl	cl	fl	gl	pl	sl
a	black	clap	flag	glad	place	slang
e	blemish	clematis	flesh	glen	please	sleep
i	bliss	cliff	flipper	glitter	pliers	slipper
o	block	clock	flop	glow	ploy	slow
u	blue	club	fluff	glue	plump	slump

	br	cr	dr	fr	gr	pr
a	brag	crack	drake	frank	grab	practical
e	bread	creak	dregs	fresh	gremlin	present
i	brick	cringe	drip	frill	grits	prim
o	broken	crop	drop	frost	grow	proper
u	bruise	crumb	drum	fruit	grub	prune

	tr
a	trap
e	treat
i	trick
o	trot
u	truck

	sc	sk		sl	sm		sn
a	scab	skate	ask	slap	small	chasm	snap
e	[1]	sketch		sled	smell		sneer
i		skip	whisk	slim	smile	prism	snip
o	Scot		kiosk	slow	smoke	microcosm	snoop
u	scum	skull	tusk	slumber	smuggle		snuggle

[1] **Sce** and **sci** words do not have two sounds. The **c** is silent.

	sp		st	
a	space	clasp	stay	fast
e	speck		step	latest
i	spider	crisp	stick	artist
o	spot		stop	lost
u	spud	cusp	stump	must

	sw	**tw**
a	swag	twang
e	sweep	twenty
i	swing	twice
o	swoop[2]	
u	swung	

[2] The combination **sw** followed by a short sound is spelled **swa**: *swan, swallow, swap*.

TEACHING TIP: Young children who are relying heavily on sound often produce strange spellings, such as *chruck* (truck) and *jrum* (drum). They are listening for all the sounds, but neither hear nor pronounce words correctly and clearly.

Combinations with c and k

TEACHING TIP: If you collect words which have **k** and words which have **ck**, and list them in two separate columns, you will see what makes the difference. (It helps to read them aloud.) You will discover that most of the time, when a short vowel immediately precedes the **k** sound, you will use **ck**.

Short vowel immediately before the **k** sound:

pack	check	tickle	locket	mukluk[1]
sack	peck	sick	clock	duck
tackle	heckle	pickle	sock	truck

[1] Note *mukluk*, a kind of boot worn in the high Arctic. The word belongs to an Inuit language.

When a short vowel does *not* immediately precede the **c** sound, you will use **k**, and rarely **c**.

Not-short vowels immediately before the **k** sound:

bank	cheek	silk	honk	dunk
park	jerk	irk	pork	chunk
ask		sink		murky
arc		zinc		
talc				

TEACHING TIP: Categorizing in this way and looking for reasons *why* words are spelled the way they are can help students make logical choices when spelling the words.

ETYMOLOGICAL NOTE

The only **kk** words you are likely to come across are *trekkie* and *trekking*, both derived from the Afrikaans word *trek*.

A double **k** is almost impossible in English. Words that sound as if they have a **kk** have **ck** instead.

packing	pecking	ticking	docking	ducking
bracket	beckon	thicket	locket	plucking
hacker	checker	sticker	knocker	trucker
bracken	heckle	chicken	clocking	shucking

Words Ending in **ic**

Words of more than one syllable are more likely to end in **ic** than in **ick**.

magic	music	poetic	Arctic	Antarctic
Atlantic	tragic	arithmetic	lunatic	magnetic
metric	plastic	graphic	dynamic	picnic
static	electric	politic	economic	atomic
eccentric	frantic	mimic	frolic	panic

Exceptions are likely to be compound words in which the **ck** is part of a one-syllable word. For example: *candlewick*.

WORDS TO NOTE

A few words end in **ac**:

shellac
bivouac
cardiac

[1] You must do this to retain the hard **c** sound. See page 92.

> **SPELLING TIP:** When adding a suffix to a word ending in **ic** or **ac**, always add a **k**:
>
> picnicking panicking frolicking mimicking
> shellacked bivouacked[1]

A **ct** Sound Problem

How can you avoid confusing these two groups of spellings?

a**ct**	se**ct**	edi**ct**	O**ct**ober	du**ct**
tra**ct**	expe**ct**	Pi**ct**	do**ct**or	dedu**ct**
tra**cked**	pe**cked**	pi**cked**	do**cked**	du**cked**
ha**cked**	de**cked**	tri**cked**	sto**cked**	plu**cked**

The sound you hear is the same. However, the words in the second group are all past-tense verbs. It is common for the **ed** ending to sound like **t**.

Similarly, it is easy to confuse the two groups below, if you do not
consider the meaning and part of speech.

a**pt**	bere**ft**	cry**pt**	ado**pt**	eru**pt**
ada**pt**	ade**pt**	dri**ft**	alo**ft**	corru**pt**

Past-tense verbs:

ca**pped**	pe**pped**	tri**pped**	to**pped**	cu**pped**
la**pped**	schle**pped**	milk**ed**	toss**ed**	rebu**ffed**

Nasal **m** and **n**

Sometimes, **m** and **n** form combinations called nasals, which are difficult
for young children to hear. Consequently they omit them.

camp	hemp	limp	stomp	bump
ramp	temper	whimper	compete	jumper
amber	remember	limber	combine	fumble
ramble	resemble	timber	sombre	rumble
and	send	mind	pond	under
candle	depend	window	sound	bundle
sang	length	ring	belong	hung
dangle	strength	swing	song	bungle
sank		think	honk	dunk
ankle		pink	plonk	skunk
ant	sent	mint	don't	hunt
want	spent	lint	won't	stunt

Three Letters — Two Sounds*

These combinations are built on digraphs: **ch**, **sh**, **th**, and more rarely **ph**. They are usually paired with **n** or **r**.

nch

ranch	bench	pinch	poncho	bunch	lynch
branch	stench	winch		lunch	

rch

march	perch	birch	porch	lurch
arch	merchant	smirch	torch	urchin

chr

Christian	chrome		chrysalis
Christmas	chromatic		chrysanthemum

shr

shrank	shred	shrink	Shropshire	shrub
shrapnel	shrewd	shrivel	shrove	shrug

thr

thrash	three	thrifty	through	thru[1]
enthrall	thread	thrill	throw	thrush

nth

panther	enthrall	ninth	month	Scunthorpe

[1] A spelling used in North American fast-food restaurants and road signs. Students need to learn when using it is appropriate and when not.

* Three-letter combinations involving silent letters are looked at on page 28.

[2] The North American pronunciation.

	Less frequent combinations:		
lch	belch	pilchard	mulch
lth	although	stealth	filth
rsh	marsh	Hershey	
phr	phrase	phrensy	phrenology
sch	scheme	school	scholar	schedule[2]

Three Letters — Three Sounds

Because all three sounds can be heard, even beginning spellers can sound out these three-letter combinations if they listen and pronounce the words carefully.

scr					
	scrap	screen	script	scroll	scrum
	scratch	screech	scribble	Scrooge	scrumptious

spr					
	sprain	spree	spring	sprocket	spruce	spry
	spray	spread	sprinkle	sprout	sprung	

str					
	strap	street	strict	astronaut	strut
	strait	streak	strip	stroke	strum

[1] Combinations with the nasal **m** and **n** are more difficult to hear, and are more liable to be misspelled.

mbl[1]				
	amble	dissemble	nimble	mumble
	gamble	resemble	thimble	fumble

mpl				
	ample	temple	simple	rumple
	sample	steeple	dimple	crumple

ndl				
	candle	spindle	fondle	bundle
	handle	kindle	soundly

Four and More Letter Combinations

These combinations are quite rare, with many of those you find being compound words. In many of the words which seem to have a long string of consonants, a **y** is used as a vowel. You may be interested in collecting words like these as you find them. Keep them in columns, according to the number of consonants together.

4	5	6
stre**ngth**	le**ngths**	wa**tchstr**ap
sy**nchr**onize[1]	bla**ckstr**ap	la**tchstr**ing
dra**ftsm**an		
la**ndsc**ape		
a**nthr**opology		
e**nthr**all		
di**phth**ong		
tou**chst**one		
ar**chb**ishop		
be**nchm**ark		

Silent Letters

One problem with silent letters is that we cannot predict their presence in a word. The only way we know a word has a silent letter is if we already know how to spell the word.

Almost every letter of the alphabet can be silent. Some letters disappear from sound as a result of sloppy pronunciation.

han**d**kerchief	parli**a**ment	fo**re**castle	February

Some silent letters are relics of words' language of origin, and pronunciation has changed while the spelling has not.

know	**k**nockwurst	**m**nemonic	**g**nome

Some letters are silent because we retain the original foreign pronunciation.

debri**s**	rende**z**vous	croche**t**	ricoche**t**

Some silent letters were deliberately introduced in a move to restore etymological links.

| reign | to link with the Latin *regnum* |
| debt | to link with the Latin *debitum* |

TEACHING TIP: First, make children aware that silent letters exist; then help them recognize the common silent-letter patterns.

SPELLING TIP: *Two* is commonly misspelled. To help remember the silent **w**, think of *two* in conjunction with *twice, twins, twelve, twenty.*

[1] *Ghastly* is derived from the same root as *ghost*.

[2] For other words in the **wh** pattern, see page 18.

SILENT LETTER PATTERNS

w	k	h	b	t
write	know	ghost	crumb	often
wrist	knew	ghastly[1]	comb	soften
wrap	knee	gherkin	limb	whistle
wriggle	knit	ghetto	thumb	thistle
wrong	knock	ghoul	climb	castle
wrestle	knife		lamb	wrestle
wrinkle	knapsack	what[2]	doubt	trestle
wrack	knave			
wraith	knickknack	rhino		
wrangle	knight	rhythm		
wrath	knob	rhyme		
wreak	knoll	rhea		
wreck	knuckle	rhubarb		
wrest		rhombus		
wretch		rhapsody		
wright				
wring				
writhe				
wroth				
wrought				
wryly				
who				

SILENT LETTER PATTERNS — *Continued*

l	g	n
calf	sign	solemn
half	align	column
walk	benign	autumn
talk	assign	condemn
chalk	consign	
stalk	malign	
	resign	

SILENT *P* PATTERNS

These words are all of Greek origin, and most have a strong connection to science and medicine. Some are prefixes which attach to many roots to form large meaning patterns. For interest's sake, take a look in a large dictionary to see just how many silent **p** words there are.

psalm	pseudo	psoriasis	psyche
psalter			psychology
pshaw			
ptarmigan	pteriodology	Ptolemy	
	pterodactyl	ptomaine	
	pteropod	ptyalin	

SILENT *GH* PATTERNS

gh	ght	
bough	sleight	caught
slough		taught
	fright	naught
though	night	fraught
	sight	
nigh	knight	bought
sigh	bight	fought
		ought
sleigh	eight	sought
weigh	freight	brought
neigh	weight	thought
through		drought

2/Vowels

Every vowel sound can be represented by several different letters or groups of letters. This is often because our words have come from many different languages, each with its own logic and pattern. Also, we are constantly changing the way we pronounce words. Spelling changes too, but far more slowly. Consequently, spelling and sound often grow farther apart over time.

Many vowel sounds depend on dialect. In different parts of the English-speaking world, the vowel sounds mainly denote regional accents. In a recent telephone call, an acquaintance in Michigan was passing on to me the name *Ann*; I heard and wrote down *Ian*.

In certain southern counties of England, *bath* and *hearth* rhyme, with the vowel sound exactly the same and the **r** undetectable; in the north of England the sounds in these two words differ markedly. In North America, *fall* and *doll* rhyme — the vowel sounds are exactly the same; in the rest of the English-speaking world they are not. Similarly, *caught* and *cot* sound identical in North America, but not in England or Australia. In parts of the United States, my English ear cannot tell the difference between the pronunciations of *center* and *sinner*.

We must each build vowel rhyming patterns according to our own dialect. As you read the words here, you can decide which, if any, do not fit in your dialect.

PRONUNCIATION NOTE

The four **e**'s in *reentered* each have a different pronunciation, including one silent one.

Short Vowels

One way to build short-vowel patterns is to write as many different spellings for the sound as possible. Next, for each spelling see how many different letters can follow or precede the vowel. Each of the words on your list may start a new group of rhyming words.

Some vowel spellings are so rare that you may find only one example. They are not worth spending much time on, but coming across them and taking note of them is interesting. If any of these rarities are words we need to write, we must to learn them as sight words. Often these stick in our minds just because we find them so unusual. Frequency of use is more effective in imprinting these on our memories than sitting down to learn them in isolation.

[1] In Scotland, the **ae** in *Gaelic* is pronounced as a short **a**; in Ireland it is pronounced as a long **a**.

a	**a**	**au**	**ai**	**i**	**ae**
	cab	laugh	plaid	meringue	Gaelic[1]
	access				
	sad				
	staff				
	stag				
	pal				
	am				
	an				
	trap				
	has				
	cat				
	have				
	axe				
	dazzle				

[2] *Leisure* can have a long **e** sound or a short **e** sound, depending on dialect.

e	**e**	**ea**	**ai**	**eo**	**ei**
	bed	bread	said	leopard	leisure[2]
	left	meant	mountain		heifer
	egg	leapt			
	trek	feather			
	bell				
	them				
	hen				
	shepherd				
	equine				
	establish				
	net				
	never				
	exit				
	Ezra				
	ay	**ie**	**ae**	**a**	**u**
	says	friend	aesthetic	any	bury
				many	

i	i	y	o	e	ui
	bib	symmetry	women	women	build
	nickel	lynx		English	
	lid	tyranny			
	skiff	physician			
	igloo				
	ill				
	important				
	inform				
	zipper				
	whisper				
	sit				
	give				
	six				
	quiz				
	ie	**u**	**ei**	**ie**	**ai**
	sieve	busy	forfeit	sieve	mountain
			foreign		

[3] These words rhyme as shown only in North America. In other dialects, *off, cough, trough* and *yacht* share the same vowel sound, while all the others share a different vowel sound.

o[3]	o	augh	ough	aw	a	au
	knob	caught	ought	jackdaw	ball	auburn
	broccoli	daughter	bought	awesome	call	faucet
	trod	taught	fought	awful	fall	auditory
	off		thought	awkward	gall	august
	log		sought	awl	hall	auk
	doll			fawn	mall	Paul
	homily				pall	launch
	fond				tall	Australia
	stop				wall	auto
	cross				squab	
	not				squad	
	hovel				quaff	
	box				qualify	
	Oz				quantity	
					quarrel	
					wander	
					watch	
					what	

ou	ah	oa	al	ach
c**ou**gh	Ut**ah**	br**oa**d	c**al**m	y**ach**t
tr**ou**gh				

You can group these **u**-words according to their different pronunciations. Be aware that many of these pronunciations are dialect-dependent.*

u	u	ou	o[4]	oo	o	u
	d**u**ck	t**ou**gh	c**o**me	w**oo**d	w**o**lf	p**u**dding
	m**u**d	en**ou**gh	s**o**me	w**oo**f	w**o**man	p**u**ll
	st**u**ff	tr**ou**ble	s**o**n	b**oo**k[5]		
	r**u**g	y**ou**ng	t**o**n	w**oo**l		
	m**u**kluk		d**o**ne			
	h**u**ll		w**o**nder			
	s**u**m		t**o**ngue			
	f**u**n		gall**o**p			
	up		m**o**ther			
	f**u**ss		l**o**ve			
	c**u**t		**o**ven			
	b**u**zz					

	oo	oi	oe	oul		
	bl**oo**d	porp**oi**se	d**oe**s	c**oul**d		
	fl**oo**d	tort**oi**se		sh**oul**d		
				w**oul**d		

[4] Much of the time, we pronounce *of* with a short **u** vowel sound. Be prepared for beginning spellers to spell the word *uv*.

[5] In certain areas of northern England, *book* is pronounced with a long **u** sound, much like the sound in *fool*.

ETYMOLOGICAL NOTE

Many words which sound as if they should have a **u** have an **o** instead. The old English for *love* was *lufu*. The change in spelling came about because William Caxton, the first printer in the English language, found that his printing press would not print a good, clean **u**, so he substituted the **o**.

* You can also consider the many different spellings of **shun** to represent a short **u** sound. For information on these, see pages 63-64.

WORDS TO NOTE

The **o** in words such as the following has a short **u** sound, called a *schwa*. The sound is due to saying the words in the easiest way.

    observe   **o**ccasion   at**o**m   **o**pinion   **o**riginal
other

The **a** in these words is also usually pronounced as a schwa:

    again   **a**lone   **a**mazing

Children who are relying on sound to spell may misspell these kinds of words.

Long Vowels

Long vowels are vowels which say their names. You can listen for the **a, e, i, o,** and **u** in these words:

face	meat	fine	coat	fuse

There are many different ways to spell each of these long-vowel sounds. Some spelling combinations are quite common, while others can be found only in a single word. Those which do not fall into groups have to be remembered as sight words. If any of them are words we use frequently, they are words worth learning. Often just using them frequently will allow us to remember the spelling.

TEACHING TIP: It usually takes two letters to represent a long-vowel sound.

    s**ea**t   m**i**n**e**

As you collect long-vowel words, note which two letters create the sound.

Note also the few long-vowel patterns which use only one vowel. Many of them are at the ends of words:

be	taxi[1]	go	radio	by
me		no	stereo	my

Some words have more than one example: *radio* and *potato* each have three single-letter, long-vowel sounds.

[1] The ending **i** is not common in English. *Taxi, maxi* and *mini* are abbreviations. **Semi** is a prefix; when it is used as an abbreviation for a truck, it is pronounced with a long i sound. *Ski* is borrowed from Norwegian.

Ways to Spell Long-Vowel Sounds

One way to build long-vowel patterns is to collect as many different ways to spell the sound as possible. Then for each spelling pattern, see how many different letters can come before or after it.

[1] There are two spellings of *gray/grey* here. *Gray* is American; *grey* is the accepted spelling everywhere else.

[2] *Tomato* has a long a only in North American English.

[3] The Irish pronunciation. In Scotland the word is pronounced with a short a.

a	a __ e	ai	eigh	ay	ey
	grace	raid	weigh	bay	obey
	lemonade	waif	eight	day	they
	strafe	Haig	freight	gay	grey
	age	rail		hay	
	stake	aim		jay	
	tale	complain		play	
	came	traipse		May	
	cane	raisin		nay	
	ape	wait		pay	
	phase	waive		gray[1]	
	gate	baize		stay	
	gave			way	
	gaze				

a	ea	eig	ei	aigh
baby	great	deign	reindeer	straight
bacon	break	reign	seine	
bagel			veil	
baker			freight	
stamen				
apron				
basin				
tomato[2]				
gravy				

ao	au	é(e)	ae
gaol	gauge	café	Gaelic[3]
		née	aeronautics
		fiancée	

e	e __ e	ea	ie	ei	ey
	grebe	beach	niece	Reid	key
	theme	read	field	Neil	donkey
	scene	leaf	believe	Sheila	
	these	league	lien	Madeira	

34

[4] Many words have **re** or **de** as prefixes. Consequently, these patterns are very common.

[5] Relating spelling to the students' names or names of famous people can help us remember.

[6] In the United States this word is often spelled *keys* as in the Florida Keys.

[7] When i__e represents a long e sound, the word most likely comes from French, and still retains the French pronunciation.

[8] Most words with the **ae** spelling are changing. It is now usual to see *archeology, paleontology,* etc. However, the salad is always *Caesar.*

e	e __ e	ea	ie	ei	ey
	complete	peak	believe	receive	
	eve	peal	frieze		
		dream	eyrie		
		bean			
		leap			
		ease			
		eat			
		breathe			
		leave			

eo	ee	e	ay	i __ e
people	bee	me	quay[6]	corniche[7]
	seed	zebra		regime
	beef	because		machine
	leek	bedazzle		prestige
	eel	before		
	seem	regurgitate[4]		
	green	rehash		
	sheep	relapse		
	knees	remake		
	beet	Phenix[5]		
	freeze	depend		
		equal		
		erase		
		evade		

ae[8]	oe	is	y	i
aegis	Phoenix	ambergris	baby	ski
archaeology	amoeba	verdigris	democracy	ravioli
palaeontology			lady	spaghetti
Caesar			stuffy	
			baggy	
			grungy	
			tacky	
			tummy	
			cranny	
			happy	
			Harry	
			sassy	
			witty	

e				wavy
				snowy
				foxy
				lazy

	ii	eigh	ee	
	Hawaii	Leigh	reed	
			reef	
			squeek	
			reel	
			queen	
			cheep	
			cheese	
			feet	
			reeve	
			sneeze	

i	i __ e	igh	ie	ye	i
	gibe	bight	die	bye	hiatus
	nice	fight	lie	dye	ibis
	ride	high	fried	lye	mica
	knife	night	tie	rye	idol
	hike	right	vie		climb
	stile	sigh			Regina
	grime	tight			Iowa
	fine				iris
	snipe				item
	wise				ivy
	site				memorize
	hive				
	energize				

y	ui	ai	aye	eye	uy
my	guide	aisle	aye	eye	buy
hybrid	guise				
hydro					
hyena					

defy					
bygone					
phylum					
myopic					
cypress					
byways					

i	y _ e	ei	igh
	style	eiderdown	nigh
	thyme	height	sigh
	type	stein	
	tyre[9]	seismic	
	analyse	either[10]	
	electrolyte		
	paralyze		

[9] *Tyre* and *analyse* are British spellings. *Paralyze* is North American.

[10] *Either* has a long i sound in England, and a long e sound in North America. See the *i before e rule* on pages 89-91.

o	oa	o _ e	o	ow	ough
	roach	lobe	koala	bow	dough
	load	ode	obituary	window	though
	loaf	poke	ocean	slow	
	oak	pole	ogle	mow	
	foal	home	okra	snow	
	foam	cone	olympic	row	
	roan	slope	omit	sow	
	soap	close	bonus	tow	
	coast	wrote	open		
	goat	wove	osier		
	loaves	owe	over		
		froze	Owen		
			ozone		

oh	ou	oe	eo	oo
oh	boulder	oboe	yeoman	brooch
doh	shoulder	doe		
soh	mould	foe		
	soul	hoe		
		Joe		
		Poe		
		roe		
		toe		
		woe		

eau	ew	au
beau	sew	mauve
plateau		

[11] The long **u** sound has at least two different pronunciations.
For example: food   feud
In some dialects, *new* has the same sound as *zoo*; in other dialects it has the same sound as *few*. We must each form our own patterns based on our individual dialects.

[12] In parts of northern England, *book, look* and *mood* share the same vowel sound.

u[11]	**oo**	**u __ e**	**ew**	**ough**	**ue**
	zoo	tube	few	through	cue
	mood	rude	lewd		due
	roof	huge	mew		hue
	book[12]	rule	newt		glue
	cool	plume	pew		revenue
	zoom	June	crew		queue
	moon	dupe	stew		rue
	loop	use			sue
	loose	lute			true
	boot				revue
	hooves				
	ooze				

u	**eu**	**ui**	**eau**	**ou**
gnu	feud	cruise	beautiful	caribou
usual	Eugene	suit		toucan
cubic	eulogy			ghoul
lucid	eunuch			Khartoum
fuel	Europe			group
bugle	eustachian			couscous
ukelele	rheumatism			youth
humid				louvre
unique				
stupid				
usual				
future				

[13] In North America *maneuver* is the spelling.

iew	**ieu**	**eue**	**ewe**	**oeu**
view	adieu	queue	ewe	manoeuvre[13]
			Crewe	

Diphthongs

In dipthongs, two vowels combine to make a new sound. You may be able to hear two vowel sounds in the new combination. In these instances, **y** and **w** are considered vowels.

oy	oy	oi
	oyster	v**oi**ce
	b**oy**	v**oi**d
	c**oy**	**oi**l
	enj**oy**	c**oi**n
	loyal	n**oi**se
	ann**oy**	c**oi**t
	sep**oy**	
	royal	
	s**oy**a	
	t**oy**	
	v**oy**age	

ow	ow	ou	ough	eo
	c**ow**	**ou**ch	b**ough**	Macl**eo**d
	cr**ow**d	l**ou**d	sl**ough**	
	sc**ow**l	s**ou**nd		
	fr**ow**n	**ou**r		
		oust		
		out		

Short Vowels and Double Letters

Short vowels and double letters have a strong relationship, often going together. This is how it works when we add endings:

	cap	capped	capping
but:	cape	caped	

This pattern helps you to read and understand words like these:

chafing	chaffing	piping	pipping
waging	wagging	sniped	snipped
wading	wadding	siting	sitting
caped	capped	lobed	lobbed
caning	canning	hoped	hopped
hated	hatted	loped	lopped

planed	planned	moping	mopping
mating	matting	sloped	slopped
riding	ridding	tubed	tubbed
rifling	riffling	luged	lugged
filed	filled	musing	mussing
dining	dinning	super	supper
griping	gripping		

As a general rule: When you add an ending to a short-vowel syllable, double the last letter. Apply this rule only when the short vowel comes directly before the last letter. It does not apply to words like these:

clasp	clasping	pick	picking
catch	catching	clock	clocking
send	sending	jump	jumping

ETYMOLOGICAL NOTE

Noah Webster introduced these spellings: *robin, wagon*.
In the English spelling of the time, these words were spelled: *robbin, waggon*, as you would predict from the short vowel–double letter pattern. In an attempt to make spelling simpler, Webster actually created two exceptions to a very useful spelling pattern.

Vowels with **ch** and **tch**

How can you tell when to use **ch** and when to use **tch**? Most words with **ch** or **tch** fall into two clear groups.

	tch	ch
a	pa**tch**	roa**ch**
	sa**tch**el	sear**ch**
	wa**tch**	ar**ch**
e	fe**tch**	mer**ch**ant
	ke**tch**up	ben**ch**
	ske**tch**	lee**ch**
i	pi**tch**er	pin**ch**
	di**tch**	pil**ch**ard
	sni**tch**	bir**ch**

o	hopsco**tch**	por**ch**
	bo**tch**	pon**ch**o
	cro**tch**ety	poo**ch**
u	bu**tch**er	bun**ch**
	clu**tch**	lur**ch**
	Du**tch**	laun**ch**

You will notice that the words on the left all have short vowels immediately before the **ch** sound. The words on the right do not. Compare this pattern with that for **ge** and **dge**.

As a general rule: When a short vowel comes immediately before the **ch** sound, use **tch**.

There are few exceptions, but some are commonly used words. Most people remember these without effort, just because they read and write them so frequently.

a	e	i	o	u
attach		rich		much
detach		which		such
bachelor		sandwich		

Aitch has a long vowel sound, but has **tch**.

TEACHING TIP: Make a collection of words belonging to each category. Try to list words using different vowels. Then look at each list, and figure out what makes them different.

Vowels with **ge** and **dge**

How can you tell when to use **ge** and when to use **dge**? Most words with **ge** or **dge** fall into two clear groups similar to those with **ch** or **tch**.

	dge	**ge**
a	ba**dge**	ra**ge**
	ba**dge**r	stran**ge**r
	ca**dge**	ca**ge**
e	e**dge**	Stonehen**ge**
	le**dge**	mer**ge**
	se**dge**	sie**ge**

i	bridge	hinge
	ridge	tinge
	fridge	dirge
o	dodge	George
	lodge	lounge
	stodge	stooge
u	fudge	huge
	budget	bulge
	nudge	urge

You will notice that the words on the left each have a short vowel immediately before the **g** sound. The words on the right do not. Compare this pattern with that for **ch** and **tch**.

As a general rule: When you write a short vowel word, use **dge**.

ETYMOLOGICAL NOTE

Privilege sounds as if it should have **dge**, but does not. It comes from the Latin **lex, legis**, meaning law. Hence the different spelling pattern. Remember the spelling by connecting it with *legal*.

Other exceptions are *pigeon* and *religion*.

Vowels with **r**

Vowels combined with **r** represent different kinds of sounds. Whether the **r** is heard clearly is often a matter of dialect. In New England, Australia, and parts of England, the words *bar* and *baa* are pronounced exactly alike.

One way to begin building a rhyming pattern is with a starter word. Choose your starter word when a word with an interesting sound pattern comes up in the course of regular classroom activities — perhaps as part of a science lesson, after reading a story, or during a writing conference. Then collect other words that share the same sound, but may have different spelling patterns. You can extend your collection by finding letters which can come before or after each group. The starter words here illustrate the rhyming patterns.

TEACHING TIP: Many of these vowel patterns create homophones (see pages 55-56) — words that sound the same, but have different spellings and different meanings. We need to focus on the meanings when spelling these words. It is a good idea to learn to spell homophones individually, rather than looking at homophone groups and trying to remember which is which.

Starter word: **car**[1]

[1] Because the sound they hear is **r**, children may at first spell this sound with just the letters **cr**, or even **kr**.

[2] The pronunciation or non-pronunciation of the **r** in words like these is different in different parts of the English-speaking world. In some dialects, all these words share the same vowel sound; in others they do not.

ar		ear	are
barley	arbor	hearth[2]	are
car	arc		
far	ardent		
hard	arm		
jar	art		
lard	starve		
marlin			
party			
sardine			
tarpaulin			
varnish			
yarn			

Starter word: **air**

[3] A British spelling, becoming archaic. Aeroplanes used to land at an aerodrome. Note the spelling of Spencer's "Faerie Queen."

air	ear	aer	eir	are
air	bear	aerial	heir	bare
fair	pear	aerobics	their	care
hair	tear	aerosol		dare
lair	wear	aerodynamics		fare
pair		aeroplane[3]		hare
stairs				glare
				mare
				spare
				square
				stare

ere	aire	e'er	ayer
there	questionnaire	ne'er	prayer
where	commissionaire		sayer

43

ear	ier	eer	ere	eir
ear	bier	beer	sincere	weir
dear	pier	deer	sphere	weird
fear	tier	cheer	mere	
gear		jeer	revere	
hear		leer	werewolf	
near		peer		
rear		career		
sear		seer		
tear		steer		
year		veer		
		eerie		

eyr
eyrie

This sound can be represented by every vowel with **r**, as well as some other letter combinations.

ar	er	ir	or	ur	yr
scholar	her	irksome	meteor	curl	satyr
burglar	mother	birth	sailor	furnace	
liar	erstwhile	fir	attorney	church	
friar	discern	quirk	worm	lurch	
bursar	perch	sir	professor	murk	

ear				ure	yrrh
earth				nature	myrrh
dearth				picture	
early					
learn					
search					

our	ere	irr		urr
courage	were	whirr		purr
ardour				
journey				
tourniquet				
saviour				
favour				

Starter word: fire

[4] *Tyre* (British) and *tire* (North American) are different spellings for the same word.

ire	igher	yre	uyer	ier
dire	higher	byre	buyer	pacifier
fire		lyre		flier
hire		pyre		crier
mire		tyre[4]		
spire				
sire				
tire				
wire				

eyer	yer	iar	oir
Meyer	dyer	diary	choir
	fryer	liar	

Starter word: or

or	ore	oar	oor	our
or	ore	oar	door	discourse
border	bore	boar	floor	four
corridor	core	hoar	spoor	valour
dory	forehead	roar		pour
for	gore	soar		your
gore	lore			
horrid	more			
sailor	Elsinore			
remorse	Singapore			
Norway	sore			
porridge	tore			
sorry	carnivore			
torpor	wore			
	yore			
	Azores			

aur	ar
aurora	war
laurel	
Mauritius	
dinosaur	
Taurus	

Starter word: **our**		
our	**ower**	**owar**
our	bower	coward
hourly	cower	
flour	dower	
sour	gower	
devour	flower	
	tower	

Starter word: **lower**	
ower	**ewer**
lower	sewer
knower	
mower	
grower	
sower	

In all patterns involving **u**, different dialects often have different pronunciations. In some of the following words you will hear a **y** sound before the **u**, and in some you will not. The difference is illustrated by the words *cure* and *poor*.

Starter word: **cure**				
ure	**ou're**	**ur**	**eur**	**ewer**
cure	you're	curious	Europe	skewer
endure		durable	heuristic	viewer
lure		jury	aneurism	sewer
pure		urine		
sure				

uir
Muir

Starter word: **poor**		
oor	**our**	**oer**
boor	dour	doer
moor	tour	
poor		

TEACHING TIP: Words with these vowel + **r** combinations can cause spelling problems for young children, because they do not hear the sounds clearly. They frequently omit the **r**, or reverse letters. For most children, eight years old is soon enough to begin to focus on these patterns, and many children will still find them difficult.

Vowels with l

Just like **r**, the letter **l** changes the sounds represented by vowels which precede it. As an example, the **ea** combination in *sea* changes when an **l** is added to make *seal*.

You can collect these according to their rhyming patterns using a starter word, and then sort out the different spellings for each sound.

Starter word: **pale**

¹ *Gaol* is an older spelling seen more in Britain. *Jail* is the common spelling in North America.

ale	ail	eil	ael	aol
ale	ail	veil	Gaelic	gaol¹
scaler	hail			
dale	jail			
regale	mail			
hale	nail			
kale	pail			
male	quail			
pale	rail			
sale	sail			
Wales	tail			
Yale				

Starter word: **eel**

eel	eal	ile	iel	ille
eel	deal	facile	field	chenille
feeling	congeal		yield	
keel	meal			
reel	peal			
	squeal			
	real			
	seal			
	teal			
	veal			
	zeal			

Starter word: **while**

ile	ial	isl	il	aisl
bile	dial	island	child	aisle
file	trial	isle	mild	
guile	vial			
while				
senile				
pile				
rile				
vile				

Starter word: **pole**					
ole	**oul**	**owl**	**oal**	**oll**	
bole	soul	bowl	coal	roll	
coleslaw			foal	toll	
doleful			goal		
hole					
mole					
pole					
vole					

Starter word: **owl**		
owl	**oul**	**owel**
owl	foul	bowel
scowl		dowel
fowl		trowel
howl		Powell
jowl		towel
		vowel

Starter word: **school**[2]

[2] In some North American dialects, *school* and *pool* are two-syllable words like *jewel*. In Britain they are not.

ool	**ule**	**ou'll**	**uel**	**oul**	**ewel**
cool	mule	you'll	duel	ghoul	jewel
school	rule		fuel		newel
pool					

ual
dual
usual

3/Confusable Spellings

Every time we write, we change words by adding different endings. Sometimes we do this to change the verb tense, as in *write* to *written*. Sometimes we do it to change the part of speech, as in *content* to *contentment*. Sometimes we change from singular to plural, as in *baby* to *babies*.

Added word endings that change the meaning or part of speech are called *suffixes*. Both the meaning and the spelling remain constant, no matter which word a suffix is added to. The suffix **ness** always denotes a noun, and means "a state of being."

Endings we add to change verb tense are called *inflections*. We commonly add **ed** to denote past tense, as in *walk* to *walked*, and **ing** to create a participle, as in *walking*.

In other European languages descended from Latin, nouns usually have a gender — masculine, feminine or neuter — and seeing any logic in these is often difficult. In French, the moon (*la lune*) is feminine, while the sun (*le soleil*) is masculine. In German, the moon (*der Mond*) is masculine, the sun (*die Sonne*) is feminine, while a woman (*das Weib*) is neuter. In post-invasion times, when several language groups were trying to communicate with one another in England, many of these inflections disappeared, thus making English easier as a second language.

Because the spelling of these endings is always the same, knowing how to use them will help us build words. In order to add them correctly we need to learn a few basic patterns:
- when to double letters
- when to drop a final **e**
- when to change a final **y** to **i***

These patterns are consistent, no matter what kind of ending we wish to add to a word. If we understand how these conventions work, we can add endings consistently without making mistakes.

* See Chapter 5, **Spelling Rules**.

Plurals

Plural endings depend on the way the singular word ends. Most plurals end with the sound of **s** or **z**.

Many beginning spellers add **z** for a plural because of the way the word sounds, for example, *dogz*. Teach them that according to the Las Vegas Rules of Spelling,* this is a **never**. No English plural is made by adding **z**.

FINAL CONSONANTS WHICH ADD *S*			ALTERNATIVE PLURAL
b	crab	crabs	
c	arc	arcs	
d	grad	grads	
f	puff	puffs	
g	bag	bags	
h			add **es**
j			no words end in j
k	pack	packs	
l	mall	malls	
m	jam	jams	
n	can	cans	
p	chop	chops	
q			no words end in **q**
r	car	cars	
s			add **es**
t	cat	cats	
v	rev	revs	
w	cow	cows	
x			add **es**
y	monkey	monkeys	
z			add **es**

* For information on the Las Vegas Rules of Spelling, see *Spelling Instruction That Makes Sense* by Jo Phenix and Doreen Scott-Dunne (Pembroke Publishers, 1991).

ES PLURALS

In the following words, you need to pronounce an extra syllable in the plural. When you hear an extra syllable, use **es**.

ch		sh		x	
peach	peaches	wash	washes	tax	taxes
bench	benches	mesh	meshes	hex	hexes
birch	birches	fish	fishes	six	sixes
porch	porches	galosh	galoshes	fox	foxes
church	churches	push	pushes	flux	fluxes

s		z	
pass	passes	waltz	waltzes
mess	messes	fez	fezzes
kiss	kisses	quiz	quizzes
loss	losses		
bus	buses/busses	buzz	buzzes

SPELLING TIP: If the final **ch** is pronounced with a **c** sound, just add **s**.

lochs   stomachs   eunuchs

You cannot hear an extra syllable, so do not need the **e**.

WORDS TO NOTE

Should you double the final **s** or **z** when making plurals? Sometimes we do, and sometimes we don't. It seems to be a matter of personal choice. *The Oxford English Dictionary* lists only *busses*, and only *gases*, while Merriam-Webster lists *buses/busses* and *gases/gasses*.

Very few words end in a single **s** or **z**. When they do, it is as if two spelling patterns are competing for attention:
1. Double the last letter when adding endings to short-vowel words: *busses, gasses*.
2. Add **es** to the word to form the plural: *buses, gases*.

IES PLURALS

In the singular these words have **y** as the final sound by itself. They all end in a consonant + **y**.

long **e** sound		long **i** sound	
baby	babies	spy	spies
pony	ponies	try	tries
fairy	fairies	fly	flies
story	stories	sky	skies
query	queries		
country	countries		
city	cities		
family	families		
theory	theories		
army	armies		
factory	factories		

WORDS TO NOTE
The plural of *money* can be
either *moneys* or *monies*.

Contrastingly, words that have the final **y** as part of the last syllable are
regular plurals adding **s**. These words all end in a vowel + **y**.

jay	jays
don**key**	donkeys
toy	toys
buoy	buoys
en**voy**	envoys
jour**ney**	journeys
tur**key**	turkeys

SPELLING TIP: For proper nouns ending in **y**, just add **s**: the two
Marys.

WORDS ENDING IN *O*

Note how many of the words which just add **s** have strong connections
with music.

Add **es**		Add **s**	
tomato	tomatoes	radio	radios
potato	potatoes	piano	pianos
echo	echoes	solo	solos
embargo	embargoes	soprano	sopranos
volcano	volcanoes	video	videos
hero	heroes	folio	folios
buffalo	buffaloes	concerto	concertos
cargo	cargoes	burro	burros
dingo	dingoes	taco	tacos
domino	dominoes	burrito	burritos
mango	mangoes	zoo	zoos
motto	mottoes	embryo	embryos
no	noes		
veto	vetoes		

Plurals spelled with either **s** or **es**:

archipelago(e)s	banjo(e)s	grotto(e)s
halo(e)s	innuendo(e)s	lasso(e)s
manifesto(e)s	memento(e)s	mosquito(e)s
portico(e)s	salvo(e)s	zero(e)s

VES PLURALS		
Some of the older **ves** endings are now disappearing in favour of a regular **s** ending.		
scarf	scarves	scarfs
wharf	wharves	wharfs
dwarf	dwarves	dwarfs[1]
calf	calves	
half	halves	
self	selves	
elf	elves	
life	lives	
wife	wives	
knife	knives	
wolf	wolves	
loaf	loaves	
hoof	hooves	hoofs
roof	rooves	roofs

[1] Disney immortalized the Seven Dwarfs, and perhaps gave us a new spelling as well.

Words that remain the same in the plural:

Note the strong animal connection.

deer	sheep	moose	elk	fish

RARE PLURALS			
goose	geese	man	men
foot	feet	child	children[2]
mouse	mice	ox	oxen
louse	lice	sphinx	sphinges
die	dice	seraph	seraphim[3]
woman	women	cherub	cherubim

[2] Children may be interested in knowing that *children* used to share its spelling pattern with *brethren* in old English.

[3] *im* plurals are Hebrew.

Foreign Plurals

In a few words, we still retain the plural endings from their original language, though in many cases we are starting to replace them with a more English-sounding **s**.

In many of these words, particularly *media* and *criteria*, people do not realize that they are using a plural word. Consequently, they do not make their subjects and verbs agree.

LATIN PLURALS	
SINGULAR	**PLURAL**
datum	data
memorandum	memoranda
medium	media
curriculum	curricula
bacterium	bacteria
alumna	alumnae
formula	formulae formulas
larva	larvae
alga	algae
alumnus	alumni
terminus	termini terminuses
fungus	fungi
cactus	cacti
stimulus	stimuli
index	indices indexes

GREEK PLURALS	
SINGULAR	**PLURAL**
criterion	criteria
phenomenon	phenomena
parenthesis	parentheses
hypothesis	hypotheses
crisis	crises

FRENCH PLURALS

In these words borrowed from French, we add **x** to form the plural in the French way. In some cases we are beginning to change the **x** to **s** to make the words fit English plural patterns.

adieux	beaux	bureaux	chateaux	gateaux
milieux	plateaux	tableaux	trousseaux	portmanteaux

ETYMOLOGICAL NOTE

Some words we use only in the plural: *scissors, pants.*

WORDS TO NOTE

mongoose   mongooses
prospectus   prospectuses

Homophones

Looking at homophone pairs together is often confusing. It is best to learn each word separately in its own meaning context. When students are thoroughly familiar with the spellings and meanings, then they can play with the words and have fun.

In English we have hundreds of homophone pairs, and some homophone triplets. In some cases, we can determine logically which spelling to choose, as the following lists will show. In other cases, mnemonic devices often help — *hear with your ear; here, there, everywhere*. The best mnemonic devices are those we create for ourselves, but sharing them with others can often help.

ETYMOLOGICAL NOTE

Homophones Words that have the same sound, but different meanings and different spellings
pair   pare   pear

Homographs Words with different meanings and different origins, but which are spelled the same
school a place of learning (from Greek)
school a group of fish (from Old English)

Homonyms A more general term covering both homophones and homographs

The words come from Greek:
homo — same; *phone* — sound; *graph* — writing; *nym* — name

---

air	heir		ant	aunt		ate	eight	
bare	bear		base	bass		be	bee	
berry	bury		blew	blue		bow	bough	
brake	break		bread	bred		by	buy	bye
capital	capitol		ceiling	sealing		cell	sell	
cent	scent	sent	cereal	serial		cheap	cheep	
cite	sight	site	coarse	course		council	counsel	
creak	creek		currant	current		earn	urn	
ewe	yew	you	fair	fare		fir	fur	
flea	flee		flour	flower		for	fore	four
foul	fowl		gnu	knew	new	grate	great	
groan	grown		hare	hair		heal	heel	he'll
hear	here		heard	herd		high	hi	
hole	whole		hour	our		its	it's	
know	no		lead	led		male	mail	

¹ In North America this word
is increasingly pronounced to
rhyme with *out* rather than in
the original French way to
sound like *root*.

meat	meet	mete	medal	meddle		one	won	
pail	pale		pain	pane		pair	pear	pare
peace	piece		plain	plane		principal	principle	
rain	reign	rein	read	reed		read	red	
right	write	rite	root	route¹		sail	sale	
scene	seen		sea	see		sew	so	sow
some	sum		son	sun		stair	stare	
stake	steak		steal	steel		tail	tale	
their	there	they're	theirs	there's		threw	through	
to	too	two	toe	tow		wail	whale	
waist	waste		ware	wear	where	way	weigh	
we	wee		weak	week		wheel	we'll	
weather	whether		we'd	weed		which	witch	
who's	whose		wood	would		your	you're	

You can sometimes choose the correct homophone by identifying the past-tense ending **ed**

aloud	allowed		band	banned		build	billed
board	bored		brood	brewed		duct	ducked
find	fined		guest	guessed		least	leased
mast	massed		mist	missed		past	passed
road	rowed	rode	side	sighed		tide	tied
toad	towed		told	tolled		trust	trussed
wade	weighed						

or the present tense ending **s**

bruise	brews	choose	chews	tax	tacks

or the adjective ending **y**

chili	chilly

or the plural ending **s**

clause	claws	close	clothes	cruise	crews
lox	locks	pause	paws	raise	rays
rose	rows	tease	teas		

Tinker, tailor, soldier, sailor,
Rich man, poor man, beggarman, thief.

The old nursery rhyme illustrates three different ways to spell an ending which appears to denote the same thing — a person who does a job. These endings can each mean "one who" or "that which." How can we know which ending to choose?

er	or	ar
teacher	sailor	beggar
worker	actor	liar
carpenter	inventor	burglar
farmer	professor	scholar
grocer	persecutor	pedlar
porter	indicator	friar
baker	distributor	registrar
brewer	educator	bursar
butcher	supervisor	vicar
defender	aviator	
waiter	radiator	
drummer	director	
haberdasher	accelerator	
robber	spectator	
fryer	investigator	
swimmer	protector	
runner	survivor	
distiller	councillor	
ironmonger	commentator	
confectioner	indicator	
refiner	fabricator	

Ar is a rare ending for this kind of word. The choice is really between the other two. Some authorities claim **er** is more common, others say **or** is more common. Whichever is the case, there is a significant number of each.

TEACHING TIP: Spelling mistakes usually occur because people use **er** when they should use **or**; it is rarely the other way round.

Words ending in **or** have a strong connection with **shun** endings.

inventor	invention	professor	profession	persecutor	persecution
indicator	indication	actor	action	distributor	distribution
educator	education	supervisor	supervision	aviator	aviation
radiator	radiation	director	direction	accelerator	acceleration
investigator	investigation	depositor	deposition		

Not all **or** words will make **shun** words, but if they do you can be fairly safe in writing **or**.*

Er words often denote an artisan or tradesperson. You can often add **y** and form the place where the activity is carried out. If you can do this, you can be fairly sure the word has an **er** ending.

[1] In the food industry, the *butchery* is the place where meat is prepared.

grocer**y**	baker**y**	brewer**y**	butcher**y**[1]
distiller**y**	haberdasher**y**	confectioner**y**	ironmonger**y**
refiner**y**			

You may also be able to recognize some other similarities. For example, **or** is often part of an **ator** ending. I see **er** words as more artisan, while **or** words belong more to the professions. Serious students of etymology might look at how many **or** words come from French, and how many **er** words come from Anglo Saxon.

Any time you can recognize similarities among words, you will be more likely to choose the right spelling.

WORDS TO NOTE

Some words can be spelled two ways, depending on the meaning:

better — comparative of good	*bettor* — one who bets
resister — one who resists	*resistor* — electrical apparatus
adapter — one who adapts	*adaptor* — electrical apparatus
conveyer — one who conveys	*conveyor* — technical equipment

No one can decide whether *conjurer* or *conjuror* is better — we use either.

---

* *Producer* is an exception to this pattern; it will make *production*. For the reason, see Rules, page 92.

Also, *porter* will change to *portion*, but these two words are not obviously connected in meaning.

ADJECTIVES ENDING IN *AR*

Note the connection with words ending in **arity**, and other derivations which can give a clue about the spelling.

angular	angularity	
circular	circularity	circulate
familiar	familiarity	
insular	insularity	
lunar	lunarity	lunatic
molar	molarity	
molecular	molecularity	
muscular	muscularity	
particular	particularity	
peculiar	peculiarity	
perpendicular	perpendicularity	
polar	polarity	
popular	popularity	
regular	regularity	
similar	similarity	
singular	singularity	
spectacular		
stellar		stellate
tubular		
vulgar	vulgarity	

ADJECTIVES ENDING IN *OR*

Note the link with words ending in **ority**.

major	majority
minor	minority
tenor	
exterior	
inferior	inferiority
anterior	
superior	superiority
ulterior	
interior	

ery-ary-ory

Grocery burglary category: How can we know which ending to choose? Categorizing the words can help.

PLACES WHERE CERTAIN JOBS ARE CARRIED OUT		
In each of these words, if you take away the final **y** you are left with the person who performs the action or makes the product.		
ery	**ary**	**ory**
bakery brewery distillery millinery confectionery pottery haberdashery ironmongery butchery grocery refinery	dispensary (dispenser)	depository

A PLACE OR GEOGRAPHIC LOCATION		
ery	**ary**	**ory**
monastery cemetery	commissary dispensary boundary library	laboratory lavatory promontory territory observatory conservatory repository depository reformatory clerestory priory pergatory

[1] For these words, look at the connection between the words ending in **shun** and the ending **or.** See page 58.

ADJECTIVES		
ery	**ary**	**ory**
	stationary	dilatory[1]
	sedentary	illusory
	discretionary	laudatory
	imaginary	mandatory
	necessary	migratory
	elementary	promissory
	primary	transitory
	secondary	admonitory
	tertiary	amatory
		ambulatory
		commendatory
		circulatory
		compensatory
		derogatory
		explanatory
		inflammatory
		obligatory
		preparatory
		respiratory
		regulatory
		congratulatory
		conciliatory
		discriminatory
		hallucinatory
		interrogatory

PEOPLE		
ery	**ary**	**ory**
	secretary	
	adversary	
	dignitary	
	luminary	

MISCELLANEOUS		
ery	**ary**	**ory**
spidery	dictionary	allegory
dysentery	statuary	category
finery	commentary	inventory
battery	burglary	oratory
bribery	vocabulary	
flattery		

For these words, think about these connections*:

spider — spidery	burglar — burglary	inventor — inventory
finer — finery		orator — oratory
batter — battery		commentator — commentary
briber — bribery		
flatter — flattery		

Very few of these **ery-ary-ory** words fit no category at all. If you know how to spell one of the words in a category, you can make a reasonable prediction about all the others. Knowing one word can help you spell many more.

efy-ify

We add **ify** to the ends of nouns or adjectives to create verbs:

horrible — horrify	beauty — beautify	signal — signify

As a verb ending, it appears in many words.

testify	certify	amplify	gratify	falsify
petrify	specify	terrify	fortify	dignify
classify	qualify	codify	pacify	rectify
ratify	modify	mystify	mummify	calcify
glorify	intensify	vilify	purify	verify

* For further clues, see **er–or–ar** on pages 57-59.

There are dozens of words which fit this pattern and only four words which quite consistently have a different spelling. If any of them are words you need to use, you must remember them as exceptions to the pattern.

liquefy	putrefy	stupefy	rarefy[1]

As three of these words come from words containing an **i** — *liquid, putrid, and stupid* — there is no logical reason why these should be exceptions to the pattern. However, if you know them, you automatically know all the rest without even having to know what they are. Always keep the number of words you have to remember as small as possible.

Shun

There are at least thirteen ways to spell the sound of **shun** at the end of a word. **Shun** is not one of them!
    Here are some patterns that emerge:

- **Tion** is the most common.
- **Chion** is the most rare. *Stanchion* is the only word in common use which ends in **chion**.
- *Fashion* and *cushion* are the only **shion** words.
- The sound of **a-shun** is almost always **ation**. Exceptions are *Dalmatian, Appalachian, crustacean* and *Eustachian*.
- *Appalachian* and *Eustachian* are the only **chian** words.
- Many of the **sion** and **sian** words have a different sound. Note the difference in sound between *mansion* and *division*, and *Russian* and *Asian*.
- **Cian** words denote a person who does a certain job. Note how many of these words derive from words ending in **ic**. (*politic — politician*).
- **Tian** and **sian** words are usually names of nationalities. You can remember at least the **ian** part by linking with Cana**dian**, Austral**ian**, etc.

TEACHING TIP: Read the Mock Turtle's Story from *Alice in Wonderland,* in which the Mock Turtle tells Alice about *uglification*. Older students will enjoy looking at the parallel structure of the words: *Ambition, Distraction, Uglification* and *Derision* — and how the *shun* endings match up with those of addition, subtraction, multiplication and division.

ETYMOLOGICAL NOTE

Falchion leapt out of my dictionary one day while I was looking for another word. A falchion was a medieval curved sword. If you don't remember this one, it will probably not be a problem. The interesting thing was, I did not forget the word, although I did not spend much time thinking about it, and until now have never needed to write it. It attracted my attention and stuck in my mind because of my interest in **shun** words, and the different ways they are spelled. It reminded me that once our awareness is raised we tend to notice words and spellings we would not otherwise be interested in. Anything we add to our store of knowledge about words has the potential to increase our ability to spell.

tion	sion	cean	shion	tian	sian
anima**tion**	ten**sion**	o**cean**	fa**shion**	Dalma**tian**	A**sian**
viola**tion**	man**sion**	crusta**cean**	cu**shion**	Mar**tian**	Polyne**sian**
collec**tion**	pen**sion**			Croa**tian**	Cauca**sian**
inspec**tion**	divi**sion**			Vene**tian**	Pari**sian**
addi**tion**	revul**sion**			Hai**tian**	Malay**sian**
subtrac**tion**	fu**sion**			Egyp**tian**	Tuni**sian**
multiplica**tion**	eva**sion**				
complica**tion**	ero**sion**				
exemp**tion**					
reduc**tion**					
deduc**tion**					
predic**tion**					

cian	cion	chian	chion	cheon	xion[1]
dieti**cian**	suspi**cion**	Appala**chian**	stan**chion**	lun**cheon**	comple**xion**
politi**cian**	coer**cion**	eusta**chian**		trun**cheon**	conne**xion**
opti**cian**				pun**cheon**	crucifi**xion**
morti**cian**					transfi**xion**
electri**cian**					flu**xion**
musi**cian**					fle**xion**
statisti**cian**					
pediatri**cian**					
estheti**cian**					

[1] Look around for instances of *connexion*, the older spelling of *connection*, in store names and book titles. *Fluction* and *flection* are now more usual spellings than those listed here.

ssian	ssion
Ru**ssian**	pa**ssion**
Pru**ssian**	se**ssion**
	mi**ssion**
	fi**ssion**

ible-able

Deciding which of these two endings is correct is often difficult. Although there are patterns, most of them have exceptions.

> **TEACHING TIP:** A good knowledge of Latin roots can help identify more patterns. However, most of us will find it more practical to collect examples and identify the main patterns, then look at the exceptions, and see if any are words we need to remember.

able added to:

Whole words	Whole words with final **e** dropped[1]	Word parts ending in **i**[2]
dependable	lovable	enviable
predictable	usable	reliable
breakable	excusable	defiable
profitable	desirable	satisfiable
agreeable	admirable	appreciable
burnable	advisable	sociable
beatable	believable	justifiable
catchable	debatable	
enjoyable	drivable	
fillable	excitable	
manageable	likable	
perishable	makable	
washable	movable	
objectionable	notable	
passable	provable	
payable	quotable	
preferable	receivable	
profitable	recyclable	
questionable	salable	
reachable	savable	
readable	servable	
regretable	sizable	
returnable	strikable	
shrinkable	valuable	
singable	presumable	
thinkable	deplorable	
lockable		
wearable		

ible added to:

Whole words	Words with final **e** dropped
contemptible	collapsible
gullible	reprehensible
resistible	sensible
flexible	
discernible	
digestible	
exhaustible	
corruptible	

able added to words ending in hard **c** or hard **g**.* If you added **ible**, the pronunciation would change.

despicable	navigable
irrevocable	indefatigable
educable	
implacable	
explicable	

able added to soft **c** and soft **g** words, but with the final **e** retained to keep the soft pronunciation.

noticeable	salvageable
enforceable	chargeable
embraceable	changeable
peaceable	manageable
replaceable	engageable
pronounceable	marriageable
serviceable	mortgageable
traceable	bridgeable

ible added to roots ending in soft **c** or soft **g**:

irascible	tangible
invincible	incorrigible
deducible	negligible
forcible	intelligible
coercible	eligible
producible	illegible

* For more about hard and soft c and g, see pages 92-93.

able or **ible** added to roots which are not whole words:

affable	arable	audible	visible
formidable	inexorable	credible	edible
unconscionable	inevitable	possible	terrible
insuperable	indomitable	horrible	feasible
potable	ineffable	compatible	infallible
portable	palpable	ostensible	
memorable	inscrutable		
probable	culpable		
malleable			

ible added to words which can add **ion**:

collect	collection	collectible[3]
connect	connection	connectible
corrupt	corruption	corruptible
access	accession	accessible
suggest	suggestion	suggestible
exhaust	exhaustion	exhaustible
contract	contraction	contractible
digest	digestion	digestible
convert	conversion	convertible
reverse	reversion	reversible
corrode	corrosion	corrodible

able added to words which can add **ion**:

predict	prediction	predictable
correct	correction	correctable
detect	detection	detectable

ible added to roots ending in **ns** or **miss**:

defensible	admissible
sensible	permissible
responsible	transmissible
comprehensible	
reprehensible	
feasible	
ostensible	

Exception: *dispensable*

sede-cede-ceed

These endings may be confused because they sound alike. Very few words have these endings, although some are used frequently:

sede	ceed	cede
super**sede**	suc**ceed**	**cede**
	pro**ceed**	ac**cede**
	ex**ceed**	re**cede**
		con**cede**
		inter**cede**
		pre**cede**
		se**cede**
		ante**cede**

ETYMOLOGICAL NOTE

Supersede is the only word in English ending in **sede**. It comes from two Latin words: **super** — above and **sedeo** — I sit. To supersede means "to sit above."

All the other words are derived from the Latin word **cedo**, I go, and have meanings related to motion.

Looking at the origins can explain why *supersede* is spelled with **s**, and all the others with **c**. However, there is no good explanation about why the others are divided into two different spelling groups. The best way to remember these is to learn the three that end in **ceed**. If you can remember these three which are probably used most often, then you will automatically know the others.

TEACHING TIPS: Create your own mnemonic. For example:

If you **proceed** to **exceed** the speed limit, you will **succeed** in getting a ticket.

It is usually unnecessary to remember all the words in a pattern. If you know the exceptions, you will know that all the other words you come across will follow the pattern.

ise-ize-yse-yze

Most of us know which words cause spelling problems for us. Choosing among these endings is one of my personal problems. I look them up constantly, and do not trust myself to get them right, partly because of differences between British and North American spelling. As I have spent half my life on each side of the Atlantic, I cannot remember most of the time which is which. At least, knowing our own weaknesses can remind us which words we need to check in our writing.

Only two common words use the **y**, along with a few not-so-common words:

NORTH AMERICAN	BRITISH
analyze	analyse[1]
paralyze	paralyse
breathalyze	breathalyse
catalyze	catalyse
electrolyze	electrolyse

[1] *Analyse*, unlike other British **yse** verbs, is widely preferred to *analyze* in Canada.

If the ending is part of the root rather than a suffix, it is likely to be **ise**:

wise	advise	rise	surprise	surmise	excise[4]	guise
likewise[2]	improvise	sunrise[3]	comprise	demise	incise	disguise
otherwise	supervise	uprise	enterprise	compromise	exercise	
	revise	arise	apprise		circumcise	
	televise					

despise	franchise	merchandise	chastise
			advertise

[2] These are all compounds built with the word *wise*.
[3] These are all compounds built with the word *rise*. Note *memorize*, *categorize*, etc., which are not compound words.
[4] These are all derived from the Latin *incisus*, to cut. Note *incision*.

ALTERNATIVE SPELLINGS

In these words, **ise** or **ize** is a suffix creating a verb. The ending **ise** is more common in Britain, while **ize** is the more general spelling in North America.

criticize	criticise
itemize	itemise
modernize	modernise
victimize	victimise
fertilize	fertilise
oxidize	oxidise
crystallize	crystallise

ALTERNATIVE SPELLINGS — *Continued*	
tranquillize	tranquillise
antagonize	antagonise
baptize	baptise
exorcize	exorcise
harmonize	harmonise
ostracize	ostracise
sympathize	sympathise
recognize	recognise
maximize	maximise
optimize	optimise
pulverize	pulverise
appetize	appetise

WORDS TO NOTE

merchandise — noun   *merchandize / merchandise* — verb
Capsize is always written with **ize**, as is *size*.

TEACHING TIP: If you wish to apply the Las Vegas Rules of Spelling,* note over 400 words end in **ize**, and only about 40 in **ise**.

* See the footnote on page 50.

ance-ence

There is a logical reason for these two endings. Words derived from first conjugation Latin verbs are generally spelled **ance**; words derived from other conjugations are generally spelled **ence**.* Many of the seemingly illogical differences in English spelling are due to words' language of origin. For most of us, who are not Latin scholars, we need to look for further help. Only one pattern works well.

If the stress is placed on the final syllable in a word ending in a vowel + **r**, **ence** is probably correct.

in**fer**	inference	in**cur**	incurrence
con**fer**	conference	re**cur**	recurrence
pre**fer**	preference	con**cur**	concurrence
re**fer**	reference	oc**cur**	occurrence
de**ter**	deterrence	ab**hor**	abhorrence
in**ter**	interrence		

* There are exceptions. For example, *resistere* gives us *resistance*.

And the pattern holds true for and these words, which sound as if they end in **r**:

re**vere**	reverence
co**here**	coherence
ad**here**	adherence

For other words, there is no obvious pattern; we just have to get used to which words belong in each group. Sometimes we can use another derivation to get a clue about whether to use **a** or **e**.

admittance	admitt**a**ble	competence	
repentance		persistence	
attendance		subsistence	
guidance	guid**a**ble	insistence	
assurance	assur**a**ble	existence	exist**e**ntial
deliverance	deliver**a**ble	prevalence	
tolerance	toler**a**te	opulence	
sufferance	suffer**a**ble	condolence	
insurance	insur**a**ble	precedence	
perseverance		dependence	
sustenance	sustain**a**ble	diffidence	
maintenance	maintain**a**ble	confidence	confid**e**ntial
reliance	reli**a**ble	influence	influ**e**ntial
extravagance		difference	differ**e**ntiate
arrogance			
observance	observ**a**tion		
contrivance	contriv**a**ble		
relevance			
acceptance	accept**a**ble		
annoyance	annoy**a**ble		

al-el-le

If the ending is added to a word, the spelling is likely to be **al**:

sign	signal	brute	brutal	arrive	arrival
commit	committal	transmit	transmittal		

As there are so many **le** words, you could look at them in different kinds of groups:

Double letter words:

paddle	kettle	little	coddle	snuggle
gaggle		fiddle	bottle	cuddle
raffle			toggle	bubble
grapple				puzzle
				scuffle

ck words:

tackle	heckle	pickle		chuckle
hackle	freckle	prickle		knuckle

Silent letter words:

castle	thistle	whistle	muscle	knuckle

Two-vowel words:

poodle	noodle	steeple	double	trouble

Nasals (combinations with **m** and **n**):

amble	tumble	candle	ankle	bangle
ramble	fumble	handle		dangle
ingle	ample	jungle		
tingle	sample	bungle		

Long vowel words:

staple	people	ogle	bugle	cycle
maple				
cable		rifle		
table		stifle		

Some of the **el** words form small groups, but most stand alone and have to be remembered.

nickel	camel	funnel	mussel
	enamel	tunnel	
		channel	
novel		kennel	
		flannel	
chapel	angel	model	barrel
			squirrel
travel	panel	label	
cancel	counsel	satchel	bushel
chancel			
parcel			

TEACHING TIP: Choose a few of these words which you use often, and print them on a card. Keep the card handy when you write, and proofread for these specific words when you are ready to edit.

ly–ally

The usual way to form adverbs is to add **ly** to adjectives.

initially	carefully	usefully	partially	vengefully
foolishly	strangely	wisely	calmly	freely
coyly				

Some words drop the final **e**. Words ending in **le** would look very strange and un-English without the **e** dropped.

	simply	singly	subtly	doubly
	amply	prickly	cuddly	bubbly
Also:	truly	duly	eerily	wholly

Adjectives ending in **y** change the **y** to **i**.

	funnily	nastily	messily	clumsily
	wearily			
Exceptions:	drily or dryly		slily or slyly	shyly
	spryly		wryly	

73

Words ending in **ic** add **ally**.

chronically   technically   basically   economically   electrically
aesthetically   historically

Exception: publicly

WORDS TO NOTE

politicly — formed from the adjective *politic*, and meaning "wise or sensible."
politically — formed from *political*, and meaning "to do with politics."
Words ending in **ll** add only **y**. Triple letters are not possible spellings in English.

dully   shrilly   fully

SPELLING TIP: A good rule is to add **ly** unless the word would look strange. Then you only need to remember the **ally** words. Many of these are built from words ending in **al**, for example, *electrical*.

WORDS TO NOTE

dicey   dicily   day   daily   gay   gaily

---

or–our

¹ British spelling.

In words for people who do something, use **or**.

actor   sailor   doctor   professor   tenor

Exception: saviour¹

Words ending in **or**:

error   squalor   horror   pallor   torpor
tremor   languor   stupor   anchor   liquor
mirror

ALTERNATIVE SPELLINGS	
AMERICAN	**BRITISH**
ardor	ardour
armor	armour
behavior	behaviour
candor	candour
clamor	clamour
color	colour
endeavor[2]	endeavour
favor	favour
flavor	flavour
fervor	fervour
glamor[3]	glamour
harbor	harbour
honor	honour
humor	humour
labor	labour
misdemeanor	misdemeanour
neighbor	neighbour
odor	odour
parlor	parlour
rigor	rigour
rumor	rumour
savior	saviour
savor	savour
splendor	splendour
tumor	tumour
valor	valour
vapor	vapour
vigor	vigour

[2] The name of the American space shuttle is spelled *Endeavour*.

[3] Not very common, even in the U.S. Perhaps the spelling does not have enough glamour.

In British English, sometimes the **u** is dropped before adding suffixes:

honorary	armorial	honorific	glamorous	coloration
laborious	humorous			

Sometimes, it is not:

honourable	colourful	humoursome	savoury
labourer	favourite	armoury	

These mainly fall into two neat groups.

Adjectives:

famous	anonymous	enormous	covetous	impetuous
spacious	poisonous	cancerous	courageous	tempestuous

Nouns:

abacus	impetus	thesaurus	circus	virus
octopus	lotus	cactus		

WORDS TO NOTE

Exceptions are some words which we still use in their Latin form. For example: *emeritus*

4/Word Building

Spelling is a word building skill.

To build words successfully, we need to understand the building blocks of language, the roots, prefixes, suffixes and inflectional endings with which all words are made. We use these word parts in many different combinations to spell any word in our vocabulary.

Children who have started out by learning to spell words on the basis of sound patterns are already skilled in word construction. They have learned to listen for the sounds of each syllable, and represent them with letters and groups of letters. After these beginning stages, learning to spell involves looking at roots, prefixes, suffixes, origins and derivations, and using these to construct words.

The ability to separate the different parts of a word can help us avoid spelling mistakes. If you can separate a prefix from a root you will never omit an **s** in *mis spell*; English has no prefix **mi**.

The more we know about the parts of words, what they mean, and how they are joined together, the better spellers we will be.

Compound Words

It is useful to be able to recognize compound words. In compound words, all the letters of both the joined words are present. Sometimes, the letter at the end of the first word is the same as the letter which starts the second word, and we may be tempted to leave one of them out.

Some double letters look strange and even wrong in compound words, especially **hh** and **kk**, as these are only possible in compound words.

hitchhiker	ranchhand	withhold
fishhook	beachhead	bathhouse
knickknack	cutthroat	outtake
roommate	dumbbell	granddaughter

WORDS TO NOTE

In a small but significant group of compound words, a letter is lost. These are compounds made with *all* and they drop one l.*

almost	already	also
altogether	although	

To collect compound words, try building them in themes using joining words like these:

TIME	WEATHER	PLACES
after	snow	over
year	rain	under
day	ice	in
night	sun	out
	thunder	up
		down

FOOD	BODY PARTS	ANIMALS	COLOURS
cake	head	horse	black
butter	hand	dragon	gold
grape	foot	fly	blue
apple	eye	dog	red
oat	ear	cat	white
pea	finger	fish	yellow
mint	hair	bug	
corn	toe	frog	
melon	tooth	monkey	
honey	wrist	snake	
berry	face	worm	

Triple compounds:

insideout	upsidedown	insofar
hereinafter	whatsoever	heretofore
thereinafter	whomsoever	
whosoever		

* See the note on adding *ful* on page 83.

Quadruple compounds:

These are probably used only in legal contexts, but do appear in the dictionary.

hereinbefore   thereinbefore

Prefixes

Words that share the same prefix are easy to locate in a dictionary, especially a Spelling Dictionary. A spelling dictionary lists only words, not definitions, origins, or any of the additional information usually found in regular dictionaries. Because of this, a group of words which share the same prefix stands out from the rest.

Students need to pay attention to the meanings of words when they look for prefixes in a dictionary, not just look at the initial group of letters. *Predict* and *prepare* share the prefix **pre**; *preach* does not.

TEACHING TIP: The word *prefix* itself has a prefix, so could be a way to introduce the concept. Then you can investigate prefixes by category.

NUMBER PREFIXES

uni/mono	one	unit	unicycle	uniform	monopoly	monarch
bi/di/du	two	bicycle	bisect	dioxide	dual	duet
tri	three	tricycle	triplet	tricorn	trillion	triple
quad/tetra	four	quadruped	quarter	quadrant	quadruple	tetrahedron
pent/quint	five	pentagon	pentathlon	Pentecost	quintuplet	quintet
sex/hex	six	sextuplet	sextet	sextant	hexagon	hexameter
hept/sept	seven	heptagon	heptameter	September	septuagenarian	
oct	eight	octet	octopus	October	octane	octave
non/nove	nine	nonagenarian	November	novena	nonagon	
dec/deci	ten	December	decade	decathlon	decimal	decibel
cent/hect	100	century	centennial	cent	centimetre	hectare
milli/kilo	1000	million	millimetre	kilometre	kilogram	kilowatt
myria	10 000	myriad				

SIZE AND AMOUNT PREFIXES

micro	small	microscope	microfilm	microphone	microcosm
macro	large	macroscope	macrobiotic	macrocosm	
magni	great	magnify	magnificent	magnum	magnitude
mega	huge	megaphone	megalith	megalomania	megaton
equi	equal	equal	equator	equation	equidistant
is	equal	isosceles	isomorphic	isotope	isometric
hyper	excessive	hyperactive	hypertension	hypercritical	hyperbole
omni	all	omnivorous	omnipotent	omnibus	omnipresent
pene	almost	peninsula	penultimate	penumbra	
poly	many	polygamy	polyester	polyglot	polysyllabic
super	greater	supernatural	Superman	supernova	superpower
ultra	beyond	ultramodern	ultraviolet	ultrasonic	ultraconservative

PREFIXES SHOWING WHERE

circu	around	circulate	circus	circumnavigate
e	out	emigrate	eject	erupt
extra	outside	extraordinary	extraterrestrial	extracurricular
im	into	immigrate	impel	import
inter	among	interrupt	intermission	international
per	through	percolate	pervade	perceive
pro	forward	propel	proceed	progress
re	back	recede	recall	retract
sub	under	subject	submarine	subcontract
super	over	supersede	superimpose	supervise
tele	far	television	telephone	telescope
trans	across	transport	transfer	translate

PREFIXES INDICATING NEGATION

a/an	not	apathy	atheist	anarchy	anonymous
il[1]	not	illegal	illegitimate	illiterate	illegible
im/in	not	immature	immobile	indecisive	indecent
ir	not	irregular	irresponsible	irrational	irreplaceable
neg/non	not	negative	neglect	nonchalant	nonsense
counter	opposite	counteract	countermand	counterrevolution	counterproposal
de/dis	opposite	deform	degrade	disagree	dishonest
un	opposite	unable	uncertain	undo	untie
for	prohibit	forbid	forgo	forsake	forswear
mis	wrong	mistake	mislead	misjudge	misplace

[1] The choice among **il**, **im**, and **ir** depends on the first letter of the root it is added to.

ETYMOLOGICAL NOTE

Flammable and *inflammable* are not opposites; they mean the same thing. This is likely because we have misused them for so long that *inflammable* has changed its meaning. Perhaps in the past people confused it with *enflame*.

PREFIX OPPOSITES					
pro	for	project	promote	propel	propose
anti	against	antisocial	antiseptic	antihistamine	antipathy
contra	against	contraband	contradict	contravene	contrary
bene	good	beneficial	benefactor	benign	benefit
mal	bad	malfunction	maladjusted	malevolent	malefactor
homo	same	homogenous	homophone	homograph	homogenize
hetero	different	heteronym	heterosexual	heterodyne	heterodox
ante	before	anterior	antebellum	antedate	antedeluvian
pre	before	prefix	prejudice	prepare	preface
pro	before	prologue	progeny	prophet	propel
post	after	posterior	postscript	postpone	postmortem
in	in	inflate	induct	intrude	invade
im	in	impel	immigrate	impose	impetus
de	out	deflate	deport	depart	depose
ex	out	exhale	exhibit	expel	excel
pro	forward	progress	proceed	propel	project
re	back	regress	recede	retreat	return
sub	under	subvert	submarine	subhuman	subordinate
super	over	supervise	supersonic	superstructure	supernatural

OTHER COMMON PREFIXES					
auto	self	automatic	autograph	autobiography	automobile
un	not	unclear	unhappy	uncover	undo
re	again	redo	replace	reaffirm	rewrite

Suffixes

There are three things to learn about suffixes:
- their meaning and/or function
- their spelling
- how to add them to words

These three things remain constant, no matter what word you add a suffix to.

	Inflectional endings denoting verb tense:			
s	gives	likes	thanks	wants
ed	thanked	wanted	liked	manufactured
en	sharpen	lengthen	weaken	frighten
ing	walking	liking	hoping	thinking

SUFFIXES DENOTING PART OF SPEECH

Noun	Verb	Adjective	Adverb
sad**ness**	harmon**ize**	lik**able**	slow**ly**
ec**ology**	advert**ise**	fest**ive**	al**ways**
friend**ship**	liber**ate**	natur**al**	clock**wise**
harp**ist**	wid**en**	child**like**	
wis**dom**	test**ify***	liter**ary**	
liveli**hood**	rav**age**	diab**etic**	
paint**er**	cov**er**	sill**y**	
capital**ism**		harm**less**	
transl**ation**		transit**ory**	
lev**ity**		pub**lic**	
judge**ment**[1]		femin**ine**	
		boy**ish**	
		circ**ular**	
		pleas**ant**	
		gull**ible**	
		cap**able**	
		talk**ative**	

[1] Often spelled *judgment*.

* See the note about exceptions on page 63.

82

REGULAR COMPARATIVES

Just add the endings.

hard	harder	hardest
kind	kinder	kindest
cool	cooler	coolest
full	fuller	fullest

Double final letter in short-vowel words.

big	bigger	biggest
hot	hotter	hottest

Drop final **e**.

safe	safer	safest
nice	nicer	nicest

Change **y** to **i**.

happy	happier	happiest
silly	sillier	silliest

IRREGULAR COMPARATIVES

good	better	best
bad	worse	the worst
some	more	the most

SUFFIXES WITH SPECIFIC MEANINGS

phobia	fear of	claustrophobia	agoraphobia	arachnophobia
ics	discipline	physics	aesthetics	politics
ite	mineral/rock	granite	bauxite	anthracite
itis	inflammation of	tonsillitis	laryngitis	arthritis
ide	chemical	bromide	peroxide	fluoride
ine	chemical	iodine	fluorine	chlorine
ose	chemical	dextrose	sucrose	glucose
ol	alcohol	methanol	glycol	ethanol

I or II?

When you add *full* or *till* to a word, drop one **l**.

painful	helpful	until
grateful	hopeful	
aweful	joyful	

THE *OLOGY* AND *IST* FAMILY

The suffix **ology** means the science, or study of. The suffix **ist** means one who practises a certain discipline.

anthropology	anthropologist	human evolution
archaeology	archaeologist	ancient relics
astrology	astrologist	horoscopes
biology	biologist	life
cardiology	cardiologist	heart
cosmology	cosmologist	universe
criminology	criminologist	crime
cryptology	cryptologist	codes
dermatology	dermatologist	skin
ecology	ecologist	environment
entomology	entomologist	insects
ethnology	ethnologist	cultures
etymology	etymologist	word origins
geology	geologist	the earth
gerontology	gerontologist	old age
hydrology	hydrologist	water
ideology	ideologist	doctrine
meteorology	meteorologist	weather
neurology	neurologist	nerves
ornithology	ornithologist	birds
paleontology	paleontologist	fossils
pathology	pathologist	diseases
pharmacology	pharmacologist	drugs
physiology	physiologist	life processes
psychology	psychologist	mind
radiology	radiologist	radiation
seismology	seismologist	earthquakes
technology	technologist	applied sciences
theology	theologist	God
toxicology	toxicologist	poisons
zoology	zoologist	animals

Roots

Roots give words their meanings. Words are constructed by combining roots, prefixes and suffixes.

We usually use the term *root word* when the root is a recognizable, whole English word. Many roots are not easily identified, as they come from other languages. Latin and Greek scholars have some advantage, as they recognize roots, their meanings, and their combining forms of spelling. Most of us, though, once we understand that words are made up of certain, reusable building blocks, can identify roots. We can best introduce young children to the concept of word building by adding affixes to whole words they know and use. Doing this can be a logical extension to building compound words.

When we add prefixes and suffixes to roots, we are building *derivations*, which can be a useful spelling strategy. In the vast majority of words, the spelling of the root does not change when derivations are constructed (except for combining forms like *divide — division*, in which the last letter changes to match pronunciation). This knowledge can help us avoid spelling errors.

REVEALING SILENT LETTERS

Note the spelling of the root in each word in the pattern. Note also how the silent letter is no longer silent in the derivations.

sign	signal	signature	insignia	designate
column	columnar	columnist		
solemn	solemnity			
autumn	autumnal			
condemn	condemnation			
muscle	muscular			
phlegm	phlegmatic			
gnostic	agnostic			
mnemonic	amnesia			

<table>
<tr><td colspan="3">CHANGE OF PRONUNCIATION</td></tr>
<tr><td colspan="3">Note that the vowels in the root do not change, even when pronunciation and stress do. (Sometimes the final letter of a root changes. These forms we have inherited from the original Latin declensions.)</td></tr>
<tr><td>pl**ea**se</td><td>pl**ea**sure</td><td>pl**ea**sant</td></tr>
<tr><td>rev**i**se</td><td>rev**i**sion</td><td></td></tr>
<tr><td>dec**i**de</td><td>dec**i**sive</td><td>dec**i**sion</td></tr>
<tr><td>der**i**de</td><td>der**i**sive</td><td>der**i**sion</td></tr>
<tr><td>conc**e**de</td><td>conc**e**ssion</td><td></td></tr>
</table>

SPELLING TIP: When you are unsure about how to spell a word, try to list one or two others built from the same root. Other words in the pattern often give information you cannot get from one word alone.

LATIN ROOTS

act	do	act	action	react	actor
aud	hear	audible	auditory	audience	audition
agri	field	agriculture	agronomist	agrarian	agronomy
amo/ami	love	amiable	amity	amatory	amateur
annu/enni	year	annual	annually	bienniel	centennial
aqua	water	aquaduct	aquatic	aqueous	aquamarine
cap	head	cap	captain	capital	decapitate
cede/ceed	go	procede	recede	succeed	antecede
dent	tooth	dental	dentist	dentifrice	trident
dict	speak	dictate	predict	contradict	dictionary
duc(t)	lead	educate	duct	conduct	aqueduct
fac	make/do	factory	manufacture	benefactor	facsimile
fer	bring	transfer	confer	refer	defer
flex/flect	bend	flexible	reflex	reflect	deflect
form	shape	form	uniform	formation	transform
grat	please	gratitude	grateful	congratulate	gratify
ject	throw	inject	projectile	reject	eject
jud/jus	law	judge	judicial	prejudice	just
liber	free	liberty	liberate	liberal	libertine
loc	place	locate	location	allocate	dislocate
lum	light	illumine	luminary	luminescent	luminous
man	hand	manual	manufacture	manuscript	manipulate
mand	order	command	demand	remand	mandate

mar	sea	maritime	marine	submarine	mariner
mem	mindful	memory	remember	memento[1]	mention
min	small	minimum	minute	minus	minor
mit/miss	send	missile	mission	transmit	dismiss
mob	move	mobile	automobile	mobility	immobile
mort	death	mortal	mortician	post mortem	mortality
mot/mov	move	motor	motion	move	motive
multi	many	multiply	multitude	multiple	multiplicity
nat	born	natal	native	nationality	innate
nov	new	novice	novel	novelty	innovate
opt	best	optimal	optimist	optimize	optimum
ped/pod	foot	pedal	pedestrian	podium	pedestal
pel/puls	drive	repel	expel	compulsion	propulsion
pens/pend	hang	suspend	pendulum	appendix	suspense
port	carry	portable	porter	transport	portmanteau
rect	straight	erect	rectangle	correct	direction
rupt	break	rupture	interrupt	erupt	abrupt
sci	know	science	conscience	conscious	scientific
sect	cut	dissect	bisect	section	sector
sens	feel	sense	sensation	sensible	sensory
sign	mark	sign	signature	signal	insignia
son	sound	sonar	sonorous	unison	sonnet
spir	breathe	respiration	inspire	conspire	spirit
spec	see	inspect	spectacles	suspect	spectator
sta	stand	stationary	statue	stabile	stagnant
struct	build	construct	destructive	instruct	structure
temp	time	tempo	temporary	temporal	contemporary
ten	hold	tenure	tenacious	tenant	retentive
terr	land	territory	terrain	terrace	terrestrial
tex	weave	texture	context	text	textile
tract	pull	tractor	subtract	attract	retract
trud/trus	push	intrude	protrude	obtrusive	abstrusive
turb	confusion	disturb	perturb	turbine	turbulent
urb	city	urban	suburb	suburban	urbane
vac	empty	vacant	vacate	vacation	vacuum
var	different	vary	various	variant	variety
vict/vinc	conquer	victory	victim	convince	invincible
vid/vis	see	video	television	visit	evidence
vit/viv	live	survive	vital	vitamin	revive

LATIN ROOTS — *Continued*

void	empty	void	devoid	avoid	avoidance
vol	wish	volunteer	volition	benevolent	malevolent
volv	roll	revolve	revolution	involve	evolve
vor	eat	carnivore	herbivore	omnivore	voracious

GREEK ROOTS

aero	air	aerial	aerobics	aeronautics	aerodynamics
arch	chief	archenemy	archbishop	monarch	oligarchy
ast	star	astronaut	astronomy	disaster	asterisk
bio	life	biology	biography	biopsy	biochemist
crat	rule	democrat	autocrat	aristocrat	bureaucrat
chron	time	chronicle	chronometer	chronic	chronological
cycl	circle	cycle	bicycle	cyclone	encyclopedia
dem	people	democracy	demography	epidemic	demagogue
gen	race	generate	genocide	progeny	genealogy
geo	earth	geography	geology	geometry	geophysical
gon	angle	pentagon	hexagon	octagon	diagonal
gram	written	diagram	grammar	epigram	telegram
graph	write	autograph	telegraph	photograph	graphic
hydr	water	hydroelectric	hydrogen	hydrant	dehydrate
log	word	prologue	epilogue	monologue	dialogue
mech	machine	mechanic	mechanize	mechanism	mechanical
meter	measuring device	thermometer	barometer	odometer	hygrometer
nym	name	homonym	synonym	acronym	pseudonym
opt	eye	optical	optometrist	optic	optician
path	feeling	sympathy	empathy	pathos	pathetic
phobia	fear	zenophobia	agoraphobia	aquaphobia	aerophobia
phon	sound	telephone	phonics	symphony	saxophone
photo	light	telephoto	photograph	photography	photosynthesis
poli	city	metropolis	police	political	cosmopolitan
phys	nature	physical	physique	physician	physicist
psych	mind	psyche	psychology	psychiatrist	psychopath
scop	see	microscope	telescope	periscope	stethoscope
soph	wise	philosopher	sophomore	sophisticated	sophist
therm	heat	thermal	thermometer	thermostat	thermos

5/Spelling Rules

No real rules apply to English spelling. English has never had an equivalent of the French Academy, which set itself up to be the guardian and arbiter of the French language.

The British Simplified Spelling Society, whose most famous member was George Bernard Shaw, has attempted, in vain, to persuade people to rationalize our spelling system. Shaw modeled both Henry Higgins and Colonel Pickering on members of that society, and the Bell's Visible Speech and Broad Romic Higgins refers to really existed. Many other famous people, including Benjamin Franklin, Charles Darwin, Andrew Carnegie and Franklin Roosevelt, have advocated a simplified, that is, more phonetic, version of spelling. The only person who has been really successful in deliberately changing spelling was Noah Webster, and like Franklin, he was motivated as much by a desire to further American independence from British customs than to do struggling spellers a favour. Even so, most of the new spellings Webster introduced in his first dictionary reverted to the British standard in the second edition, because the general public was not prepared to use them.

Having recognized the lack of official rules, we can pick out a number of spelling conventions which are regular enough to pass as rules, and which can help us prevent spelling errors. For this reason, we should know about them.

i before e

The rule about **i** before **e** only works in syllables with a long **e** sound. Therefore, the rule with the least number of exceptions runs as follows:

> **i** before **e**
> when it sounds like **e**
> except after **c**

IE WORDS

Long e

believe	field	piece
achieve	yield	niece
relieve	shield	
grieve		liege
	thief	siege
	brief	
fiend	grief	pier
	chief	pierce
priest		fierce
	shriek	
rabies[1]		
scabies		
	Riesling	

TEACHING TIP: *Friend* does not fit any of these patterns. Many people use a mnemonic like *friend to the end* to remember this one.

EI WORDS

Long e after c

receive	receipt	ceiling
deceive	deceit	
conceive	conceit	
perceive		

Long a

inveigle[2]	deign	heinous
inveigh	feign	
weigh	reign	weight
sleigh		freight
neigh	rein	eight
neighbour	vein	
		sheikh[3]
	heir	
chow mein		skein

[2] In the United States this word is occasionally pronounced with a long e sound, but *Merriam-Webster's* lists long **a** as the preferred pronunciation.

[3] Sometimes pronounced *sheek*.

EI WORDS — *Continued*		
Long i		
Fahrenheit	height	leitmotif
seismic	sleight	stein
Short i		
forfeit	surfeit	counterfeit
foreign	sovereign	

EXCEPTIONS TO THE RULE

Long e		
protein	weir	seize
caffeine	weird	
codeine		

Long e after c

species

All names seem to be exceptions.

Sheila	Keith	Reid
Neil	O'Neil	Madeira

WORDS TO NOTE

When *either* and *neither* are pronounced in the British way (long **i** sound) they conform to the rule. When they are pronounced in the American way (long **e**), they are exceptions. Similarly, when *leisure* is pronounced in the British way (short **e**), it fits the rule. When it is pronounced in the American way (long **e**), it becomes an exception. Changes in pronunciation can create spelling problems.

[4] In *science* you can hear both vowels, so you do not need a rule to follow.

OTHER *IE* WORDS

These kinds of words do not fit the patterns above, because the **ie** is not a vowel combination. To spell these correctly you need to focus on adding the appropriate ending.

ier	ient	ience/iency	ery
fancier	efficient	efficiency	fiery
financier	deficient	deficiency	
cashier	sufficient	sufficiency	
frontier	ancient		
	patient	patience	
	quotient		
	prescient	prescience	
		conscience	
		science[4]	

i, y and e soften c and g

ce	ci	cy	ca	co	cu
cedar	cicada	cygnet	cabin	cobble	cup
cerebral	civil	cybernaut	cat	cord	cupola
Celsius	cinder	cynic	carnivore	cooper	custard

ge	gi	gy	ga	go	gu
geriatric	giblet	gypsy	gale	gone	guppy
gerbil	ginger	gyro	gasp	gondola	gum
gender	Regina	gymnast	gallivant	goose	regular

This useful pattern can help us avoid many spelling mistakes. However, you may want to start a collection of exceptions. There are more exceptions in **g** words.

get	gill[1]	gynecology
tiger	gift	
	giggle	
	Gilbert	
	girth	

[1] This is pronounced with a soft **g** when it is a liquid measure, and with a hard **g** when it is part of a fish. A liquid gill is either a quarter or half a pint, depending where in England you live.

This pattern can supersede other patterns. For example: It is usual to drop a final **e** before adding endings beginning with vowels:

recognize	recognizable	grate	grating

If you dropped the final **e** in the following words, though, you would lose the soft **c** and soft **g**.

notice	(noticable)	courage	(couragous)

To maintain the soft **c** and **g** sounds, we must keep the final **e**.

replaceable	changeable
noticeable	courageous
pronounceable	marriageable
serviceable	advantageous
traceable	salvageable

peaceable	gorgeous
enforceable	outrageous
bounceable	mortgageable

This pattern explains why we have a silent **u** in words like the following. It is to maintain the hard **g** sound.

guest	guilt	guy
guerilla	guide	Guyana
Guernsey	intrigue	
guess	guild	
Guelph	guinea	
	guitar	
	guile	
	guise	
	disguise	

Change **y** to **i**

When the **y** is a syllable by itself, change **y** to **i**.

happy	happiness	happily		
carry	carried	carrier		
cry	cries			
lady	ladies			
vary	variable	variant	variance	variety
ally	allied	alliance		
try	trier	trial		
silly	silliness			

Never create a word with **ii**. Keep the final **y** instead.

try	trying	cry	crying
spy	spying	defy	defying
vary	varying	ally	allying
satisfy	satisfying	unify	unifying

When **y** is part of the final syllable, leave it intact.

delay	delayed	delaying		
relay	relayed	relaying		
convey	conveyed	conveying	conveyance	conveyer
grey	greyed	greying	greyer	
enjoy	enjoyed	enjoying	enjoyable	enjoyment
annoy	annoyed	annoying	annoyance	
buy	buyer	buying		

SPELLING TIP: Words like *ladylike* and *handyman* are compound words, not roots with suffixes added. Therefore, all the letters of the joined words are present.

Drop the final **e**

It is more usual to drop the final **e** when adding a suffix beginning with a vowel. If you did not, the word would probably look strange.

[1] Here the **y** is used as a vowel.

[2] The final **e** is sometimes retained before a suffix beginning with **a**, as in *noticeable*. See page 66.

change	changed	changing		
admire	admired	admiring	admirable	admiration
bone	boned	bony[1]		
use	usable[2]			
culture	cultured	culturing	cultural	
desire	desired	desiring	desirous	desirable
wide	wider	widen		
ride	rider	riding	ridable	
refine	refined	refining	refinable	refinery
rise	risen	rising		
nerve	nervous	unnerving		
note	noted	noting	notable	notation

Keep the final **e** when adding a suffix beginning with a consonant.

awe	awesome	
use	useful	useless
safe	safety	
nice	nicely	
strange	strangely	strangeness